"At last a book that not only counsels us to 'let go' but that tells us exactly how to do it. . . . Here's a book that can make a real difference in our daily lives, not just in our heads."

— HAL ZINA BENNETT, author of *Write from the Heart* and twenty-eight other books on creativity and spiritual development

"Reading this, I am struck once again by Hugh Prather's down-to-earth brilliance. Letting go—particularly of fear—has been my desire and goal for years. With the help of this book, I am finally beginning to do it!"

— M. J. RYAN, author of *Attitudes of Gratitude* and *365 Health and Happiness Boosters* and editor of *The Grateful Heart*

"Ah, the freedom gained from releasing old, inhibiting stuff! The dream of such freedom can become a reality with the help of the Hugh Prather's wonderful *Little Book of Letting Go.*"

— SUE PATTON THOELE, author of *The Courage to Be Yourself, Freedoms After 50,* and *The Woman's Book of Soul*

"Letting Go is the key to happiness, success, and all the positive aspects of life. Please do yourself a favor and read it. Then practice it. I guarantee it works, if you work it."

— WALLY AMOS, author of *Watermelon Magic*

"Practical while being humorous, this book addresses the most common of human struggles while offering ways to lift the soul to all it is capable of."

— LEE L. JAMPOLSKY, PH.D., psychologist and author of *Healing the Addictive Mind* and *Smile for No Good Reason*

"*The Little Book of Letting Go* leads to the 'big heart of loving.'"

—WILLIAM ELLIOTT, author of *Tying Rocks to Clouds*

"This book brings wit, wisdom, insight, and practical help into some of life's most difficult attachments. "Letting go" seems to be the most difficult thing in life to do. But, with this book, you not only see the wisdom in doing so, you are also given the tools that will facilitate the process."

—BEVERLY HUTCHINSON, Founder and Director of Miracle Distribution Center

"In his masterful style, Hugh Prather has once again presented a way to a deeper happiness. Put this book into practice and you will have "the twinkly heart of a child."

—BARRY AND JOYCE VISSELL, authors of *The Heart's Wisdom* and *Meant to Be*

the
Little
book of
Letting
go

Other Hugh and Gayle Prather Titles
That Supplement *The Little Book of Letting Go*

Spiritual Notes to Myself:
Essential Wisdom for the 21st Century
CONARI PRESS

Spiritual Parenting
HARMONY BOOKS

I Will Never Leave You:
How Couples Can Achieve the Power of Lasting Love
BANTAM BOOKS

Notes to Myself:
20th Anniversary Edition
BANTAM BOOKS

the Little book of Letting go

A Revolutionary 30-Day Program
to Cleanse your Mind, Lift your Spirit
and Replenish your Soul

HUGH PRATHER

Foreword by Gerald G. Jampolsky, M.D.

 CONARI PRESS

First published in 2000 by
Conari Press
Distributed by Red Wheel/Weiser, LLC
York Beach, ME
With offices at:
368 Congress Street
Boston, MA 02210
www.redwheelweiser.com

ISBN: 1-57324-503-8

Cover and Book Design: Suzanne Albertson

Library of Congress Cataloging-in-Publication Data

Prather, Hugh.
    The little book of letting go : a revolutionary 30 day program to cleanse your mind, lift your spirit, and replenish your soul / Hugh Prather.
        p.   cm.
    ISBN 1-57324-503-8 (trade paper)
    1. Peace of mind. 2. Peace of mind—Problems, exercises, etc.
    I. Title.

BF637.P3 P73 2000
158—dc21   00-022063

Printed in the United States of America on recycled paper.

02 03 04 05   RRD   10 9 8 7 6 5 4 3 2

To Gayle with love

(As with all our books, this was a team
effort. Gayle contributed the title, the
theme, and worked out most of the
concepts. I did the writing.)

the Little book of Letting go

Illustrative Stories

In most instances, identifying details have been altered in these stories as well as throughout this book to protect the identity of the individuals mentioned. Three of these stories have appeared in previous books.

Foreword

by Gerald G. Jampolsky, M.D.,
author of *Love Is Letting Go of Fear*

I s anything more important than learning to experience ourselves as whole and as the essence of Love? I cannot think of anything, and Hugh Prather has written a simple, clear book that presents practical ways to let go of the blocks that interfere with experiencing our natural state of wholeness, joy, peace, and oneness with our Creator. The stories in this book, which are honest and deeply affecting, leave readers with the kind of "Ah ha" awareness that allows for spiritual transformation.

I have known Hugh and Gayle for more than twenty-two years and cherish the deep, loving friendship that we have. I have witnessed their humanness, trials, errors, and tribulations, and, as for most of us, life has not always been easy for them. But through these years, I have also witnessed their absolute commitment to their spiritual journey and to those who come to them for help.

As he always does, Hugh writes with humor and clarity about the ordinary, mundane problems that most of us struggle with. While deeply spiritual in tone, his writing tends to stay away from the kind of religious terminology that can separate rather than unite. Above all, this is a practical book, with practical solutions for everyday difficulties. It is not an abstract book of impressive-sounding concepts, but one that is filled with the precious spiritual nuggets that can lead us to a life filled with love and hope. It is a book about healing our fear of intimacy and our fear of love and happiness.

Hugh makes it absolutely clear that life does not have to be as complicated as we usually make it. He brings freshness and candor to ancient insights and leaves the reader free to ponder, disagree with, and especially to reexamine old beliefs, habits, and thoughts. When we finally realize that letting go of what has no value is not a sacrifice but the road to our personal freedom and happiness, we will embrace the practices that allow us to accomplish this. The "Releases" in this book are a way to freedom from the judgments, thoughts, and attitudes that poison our minds and lives. They will help readers become more conscious of their feelings and thoughts as a preparation to freeing their minds and becoming whole.

Letting go is an ongoing process that must be mastered, and while the writing in this book is clear, concise, and easy to read, it does require readers to participate in their liberation. The value of these Releases is priceless because they open the door to freedom from the bondage of negative, fearful thinking and set hearts and minds free to soar with the wings of peace, unity, and happiness.

The last chapter of this book is a powerful, poetic description of the benefits of letting go, surrendering to love, and finally taking that leap of faith to trust God as our guide through the pathways of life. The result is a joy and peace that defies both imagination and comparison.

This is a great, must-read book.

The River and the Lion

After the great rains, the lion was faced with crossing the river that had encircled him. Swimming was not in his nature, but it was either cross or die. The lion roared and charged the river, almost drowning before he retreated. Many more times he attacked the water, and each time he failed to cross. Exhausted, the lion lay down, and in his quietness he heard the river say, "Never fight what isn't here."

Cautiously, the lion looked up and asked, "What isn't here?"

"Your enemy isn't here," answered the river. "Just as you are a lion, I am merely a river."

Now the lion sat very still and studied the ways of the river. After a while, he walked to where a certain current brushed against the shore, and stepping in, floated to the other side.

Letting Go: The Basics

Within the human heart, we all feel the call to be simple, to be present, to be real. Yet throughout the day, the world urges us to be at war with ourselves and each other: "Be resentful about the past." "Be anxious about the future." "Be hungry for what you don't see." "Be dissatisfied with what you do see." "Be guilty." "Be important." "Be bored." "Be right." Little else in nature exhibits this need to be more than it is. The simplicity of rain, the clarity of a star, the effortlessness of a bird, the single-mindedness of an ant—all are just what they are.

Underwear on the floor can break up a marriage. Yet the eyes of puppies light up when they see boxers or briefs. To them, dirty socks are not reasons for fights but reasons for play. Obviously, most little animals are hooked on something quite divine. Something within them releases enormous freedom. I suggest that something is simplicity and purity, and that we can experience the possibilities of this natural state as well. A mind that learns to let go gradually returns to its inherent wholeness, happiness, and simplicity.

For example, the people who are in our lives today, are in our lives today—what could be simpler than this? Yet so often we react to those we encounter with a mind churning in conflict: we don't want them here; we can think of other people we would rather have here; we're not even sure we want to be here; when will this be over; why does this always happen to us; and on and on. When we become preoccupied with what we want or don't want from someone, or what we do or don't approve of, we fail to see that person's goodness, malice, gentleness, sadness, or anything else that is present. This habitual reaction to other people and to everything else in life needlessly complicates our lives and blocks simple enjoyment and peace.

Big Truck

When Gayle's and my son, John, was two years old, we lived in Santa Fe, New Mexico. One day he and I were standing on a street corner, waiting for the light to change, when a semi slowly began rounding the corner just as the walk light came on. Suddenly I was caught up in the delay this truck was causing by passing in front of us. Then I heard John say, "B i g t r u c k." I looked down and his eyes were wide with amazement. I looked at this enormous semi passing so close we could have reached it in one step. And I said, "B i g t r u c k." Because now I really saw it. It seemed like the mother ship in a *Star Wars* movie.

Maybe I'd been thinking that the truck shouldn't have been there or that what I had to do was more important than what the truck driver had to do. Whatever it was, that thought was all it took to keep me from enjoying just standing beside my son and holding his hand. Just one unnecessary thought. Little children have very few, if any, unnecessary thoughts, and that's why they are usually focused, present, and happy.

A mother bird sees a snake climbing her tree and thinks "s n a k e." Immediately she starts dive-bombing it. I have seen what a bird can do to a snake that doesn't climb down fast enough. However, it's clear what would happen to her babies if that same mother bird saw the snake and thought, "I do more good in the world than that snake." Or, "I don't like that snake; it's slimy looking." Or, "A snake in the grass has no business being in a tree." Or, "I'm going to give that snake a piece of my mind."

Not only do we give people a piece of our mind, we give them a piece of our happiness, wholeness, focus, and sometimes, a piece of our health.

> A still mind sees what is here. A busy mind sees what is not here. The one who is present is nothing more or less than the one who is present. Therefore, look at the person who is here. We can cover that person with whatever thoughts we wish, but that won't get us a different individual.

Our lives are filled with useless battles because our minds are filled with useless thoughts. We never finish thinking about anything. We carry around unhappy scenes from the past as if they were still happening, and we chew on the memory of whatever we just did. This glut of thoughts profoundly affects the world we perceive and the life we live. A man who sees his mother in every woman he meets can't see the women he meets. This one unnecessary thought lands him in solitary confinement and assures he will die alone. A mother who can't accept her son-in-law into her heart because he has "a lot of metal" (say, double earrings, a nose stud, and something rumored to be somewhere else) merely attacks her own capacity to love and be happy. She doesn't change the son-in-law and she doesn't eradicate her daughter's love for him. Yet this one unnecessary thought means her daughter will not have the mother she needs.

These last two are somewhat poisonous examples of what happens when we don't let go. Yet throughout each day, failure to let go can eat up every small chance we have to be happy. Just trying to write this page has been a typical example.

Weenies

About an hour ago, our son Jordan asked me if I could fix him "weenies the way Mother fixes them." I stopped writing and headed into the kitchen where John, who is now twenty, asked me if I could look at a business proposal he had outlined for his managerial accounting class. Gayle, being a banker's daughter, ordinarily would handle this one too, but she's at Trader Joe's buying organic yogurt.

"As soon as I fix Jordan's weenies," I said.

"Oh," John said, "would you fix me some too?"

"Yes," I said, through only gently clenched teeth.

Seasoned with my ambivalence over having been asked to stop writing about kindness and peace and actually practice them, the free-range weenies soon were simmering away in free-range chicken broth—oxymorons cooking in an oxymoron watched over by a large oxymoron.

So there I was thinking about how I wasn't getting to do

what I wanted to do; wondering where Gayle and I went wrong if our boys couldn't fix their own weenies; thinking it was a good thing we were on record against forcing kids to be vegetarians; and debating whether a dead free-range chicken was more spiritual than a dead chicken.

In a sense, we all have two minds—one whole and peaceful, the other, fragmented and busy. I was definitely in my busy mind. Just then I remembered Gayle's final words as she headed out the door: "I think we should say in the book, 'Make your state of mind more important than what you are doing.'"

Oh.

And maybe apply that to ourselves as well?

> *If it were possible to summarize all mystical teachings in a single sentence, this one would come close: Make your state of mind more important than what you are doing.*

I have practiced letting go enough to know that it feels a whole lot better than not letting go. Although my mental state wasn't too bad, it was not whole, happy, or at peace. Why must even this little bit of misery be endured? Why can't a couple of small tasks be done happily?

My mistake was the one Gayle indicated. I had made circumstances more important than my state of mind. Now I had to reverse that. I had to let go. In my experience of this process, I've come to see that it involves three steps:

The first step of letting go: *To remove what obstructs your experience of wholeness and peace, you must first look at the obstruction.*

Well, I wasn't out-and-out upset about the weenies, but I was a little resentful about what I was not getting to do, and a little conflicted about what I was doing. As I went deeper into these feelings, I found the obstructing thought: "I shouldn't have to do what I don't want to do." I looked at that idea for a moment and realized I didn't even believe it. I do things all the time I don't want to do. In this case I wanted to fix my boys this food and I wanted to read John's proposal.

Check off step 1.

Before we go to step 2, I want to emphasize one aspect of letting go that is crucial to its success. In seeking clarity about what I wanted, I would have sabotaged the entire letting-go process if I had slipped into wanting my boys, Gayle, or the situation to change.

The moment I think, "I shouldn't be fixing these weenies," all I can do is wait to be saved from the weenies. Maybe the electricity will go off and I can announce, "I tried, boys, but there's nothing I can do about it." Then I can shake my head in frustration and go back to my writing. Or perhaps Gayle will get back early and take over. Or maybe John will come into the kitchen and say, "Dad, you've been cooking weenies all your life. I think it's time I took over. You go back to writing."

Whenever our desire is for people to change or circumstances to go our way, we are not taking responsibility for our state of mind. Because now all we can do is be a victim and wait to be saved. We obviously can't let go if we are waiting to be saved. Certainly there are real victims, but most of us put ourselves in this role needlessly. And we do it every day.

When our goal is to maintain our sense of wholeness and connectedness regardless of what the day throws at us, we simply will not become a victim. Nothing is "beyond our control" because we are not interested in control. We let the people and situations we encounter be who and what they are. We are not motivated to reform or remake them. This doesn't mean we like how everyone behaves, nor does it mean that we fail to protect ourselves and loved ones from destructive people. But if we commit ourselves to changing even pleasant people when they don't want to change, we instantly become victims of their reactions. Each little response to our efforts pulls at the strings of our emotions.

For example, possibly you have been amazed, as I often have, by how frequently drivers put themselves in danger just to teach another driver a lesson. They will speed up to let someone know that he or she should not be cutting in line. They will tailgate a driver who is going too slowly. They will "run up the back" of a driver who just dangerously entered traffic. They will cut off someone who just cut them off.

Those who take it upon themselves to reform the driving public are classic victims. They have a good commute or a good trip only to the degree that other drivers act like they got the message. But other drivers never get the message.

No one has ever been made more sensitive or more thoughtful by being judged, bullied, or frightened. Putting pressure on others doesn't change their hearts. It merely engages us in a pointless conflict that splits our mind and muddles our emotions

The second step of letting go: *To go beyond the obstruction, you must be certain that you want to.*

This was easy. I wanted to cook weenies in peace. I wanted to grant a simple request from my boys in peace. I wanted to be able to break with my personal agenda in peace. I indeed wanted peace more than I wanted the thought that was obstructing peace. I took a moment to probe my honesty about all of that. I found it was pretty solid.

Check off step 2.

The third step of letting go: *To experience your wholeness, you must respond from your whole mind and not from your conflicted mind.*

To do this, I had to find the place of wholeness within me. This is an attribute of the heart that we all possess. It is the place where we feel a quiet and loving connection to others. Even though it is always there, if your mind holds a disrupting thought, and if the first two steps are not done honestly, you simply will not feel wholeness or any real connection with other people. But if you are able to go to what has been called "the place of beauty," then you must respond from this place—and you must resolve not to slip back into your old, conflicted state of mind.

And what is the nature of this "resolve"?

It is simple sincerity. Do we sincerely want oneness and equality with those around us? Do we sincerely want to look at our life in peace? Do we sincerely want a mind that knows stillness, wholeness, and a deep bond with our partner, children, parents, siblings, and friends? Or would we rather hold back our heart just a little? Would we actually like to remain in position to judge, triumph, and be right?

Here's where the third step can get a little tricky: The process of letting go of your more destructive emotions and darker impulses does not require tight control of the subject matter of your thoughts, although most people think it does. In fact, it doesn't require control of your thoughts or feelings in any way. You are not at war with circumstances, your behavior, other people's behavior, your feelings, other people's feelings, your thoughts, or other people's thoughts. You simply are not at war. It is just the reverse. Letting go is freedom. When you find yourself in a useless battle, you merely walk off the battlefield.

An illustration of how this third step works can be found in the way we experience love. All of us have seen examples of the disastrous results of people deciding to have or adopt a child because they want someone who will love them. The reason this doesn't work is that the child has to act like the image of the child that the parent expected. But the child is her own person and acts like herself, so the war begins—and war never feels like love. Similarly, people who decide to get a dog or cat for the same reason end up making themselves unhappy. Inevitably, the pet will disappoint.

Those two scenarios are common enough that many people see the mistake. Yet when it comes to romantic relationships, they don't question their desire to find someone who will cherish them, think they are wonderful, share their interests, meet their needs, have eyes only for them, and adore them even in old age. But that doesn't work either, as our divorce rate shows.

There are many people who love gardening so much that they spend significant parts of their day watering, feeding, weeding, pruning, transplanting, and the like. And they feel adequately blessed by every effort they make. It's a pleasure to walk in a garden that someone truly loves.

How do these blessed "relationships" between person and plant come about? It would be absurd to suggest that they happen the way we are now telling ourselves romantic relations should work—the person who wants a garden looks for one that is astrologically correct, that is the right age, the right shape, that had the right upbringing, one that will be lots of fun and meet all the gardener's needs.

The reason a garden "blesses" a gardener, a pet blesses a pet owner, a child blesses a parent, and a spouse blesses a spouse is that we feel love; we have the experience of love. But we have that experience only when we ourselves love. If you don't love, the most devoted pet, child, or lover will not lay one finger on your heart—it just doesn't work that way.

> *For thousands of years, in song, sonnet, and scripture, we have been told that love feels wonderful. Most people assume this means that being loved feels wonderful. And it does. But*

> before you can know "that loving feeling," first
> you must love. When you love, you receive far
> more than the feeling of being loved. The apostle
> John said, "Love one another, because love is of
> God. And everyone who loves is born of God and
> knows God. But the unloving know nothing of
> God, for God is love."

Because it is a fact that when people love, they immerse themselves in the experience of love, we can find parents all around
us who feel deeply, blessedly loved by their damaged children,
their genetically confused pets, and their overweight partners.
We can find couples so old that they are shriveled who see and
feel the beauty of love pouring like sunlight from each other's
bodies. For this to happen, all you need to do is respond from
your quiet, united, loving mind, not from your busy, fragmented, disconnected mind.

Please understand that none of us jumps straight from a
conflicted approach to life to one of pure unity and peace. That
of course is the choice, but, realistically, we are either heading
in the direction of one or the other. We can have a growing
sense of inner wholeness and be increasingly at peace with our
life and the people in it, but we will have not-so-good days and
many not-so-good moments. All we can do is the best we can
today. It is the direction of our life that matters, not whether
we have reached some perfect stage of letting go. It is enough
to make a little progress each day. This is a more encouraging
and productive goal than attempting achievement.

I have often used the following story to illustrate the
effects of responding from wholeness as compared to
responding from conflict.

Running in the Hall

Gayle and I were leaving a gymnasium where we had just watched our son Jordan play basketball. As we walked down the long hall toward the exit, three eight-year-old girls came running past, animatedly talking and laughing. As they passed the man in front of us, he harshly yelled, "Don't run in the hall!"

This slowed them almost to a stop. They were obviously confused about why they couldn't run in this virtually indestructible hallway.

When we caught up to them, the man was almost out of sight, and Gayle said, "He didn't say you couldn't skip!"

The girls immediately started laughing and skipping down the hall. We could hear them say, "No, he didn't say we couldn't skip!"

Gayle, as she so often does around children, saw these girls' core of innocence and fun and simply responded from her whole mind. If she had been judgmental of the man and said to them, "What a grouch. I think you should run if you want to," the girls might have started running again, but they would have run defiantly or fearfully and not with the lightness of heart they had before. Although their speed would have increased, their minds would have been conflicted and uncertain.

In practical terms, responding from our whole mind means that the problems that are important to others, especially our loved ones, are important to us. For instance, a parent who loves a child does not look down on or dismiss that child's fear of thunder. If we consistently felt our oneness with our partner, we would never look down on our partner's money fears, driving or flying fears, aging fears, or fear of embarrassment. If your reaction to your partner's fear—or any other form of distress—is disdain or irritation, you do not want oneness or even friendship with your partner at that moment. To claim that our desire is to nourish our bond with another and then to turn around and act from separateness is simple hypocrisy. First we have to admit that we cherish our separateness and look long and honestly at that fact. Then we have to find that place in us where our feelings are deeply our own. It is a place of oneness and happiness, and from there we extend outwards what is changeless about us.

Letting Go of Problems

It has taken longer to describe the process of letting go than it sometimes takes to do it. In real time, it can be more like: "I don't have to feel this way. Here's how I want to feel." And then the weenies are cooked in peace. (Which is what eventually happened.)

You don't have to "feel this way," because these are your feelings. One quick, honest look at them is occasionally all that's needed to remind you of that place where you can gently lay your conflicts and concerns. Usually a great deal more is needed—hence this book. We have gotten so caught up in our feelings of righteousness, put-upon-ness, irritation, cynicism, and the like that we have forgotten we can even feel another way. As a people we have come very close to entirely losing our belief in love that lasts, commitment that doesn't waver, and peace that cannot be disrupted.

At first, letting go can appear to be a daunting if not hopeless task. Our life and world are littered with endless problems, all of which we think we would dearly love to let go of, yet seldom is even one difficulty released completely. Everyone, it seems, moves from one problem to the next with no real season of rest. Even in the course of a single day, "it's just one thing after another."

So central are difficulties to the meaning of people's lives that we usually define the individuals around us by their problems. Notice this the next time you hear someone who isn't present being discussed. Whether positively or negatively, their problems are being highlighted. This is true of our own self-definition as well. We tend to think of our identity, and even the overall meaning of our life, in terms of the difficulties we encounter.

We also believe we can gauge how severe other people's problems truly are, yet what might be a minor problem to one person can preoccupy another. There are two neighborhood cats, born and raised in the wild, who have adopted us. They love us so much that they bring us a portion of every bird, rat, and lizard they kill. Cleaning up these gifts is not a problem for me, but when I am out of town, it's a problem for the rest of my family. On the other hand, I would have to concentrate very hard to exchange e-mail with certain people in peace. Yet Gayle handles this task in stride.

It isn't that some people have a truly difficult life while others get off scot-free. We have all seen individuals go through shocking tragedies in relative peace, and we have seen ourselves and others eaten up by the daily grind. Enough happens in the course of a normal day—that is, there is enough raw material for the mind to work on—for any of us to justify being unhappy.

> *Problems assault us to the degree they preoccupy us. The key to release, rest, and inner freedom is not the elimination of all external difficulties. It is letting go of our pattern of reactions to those difficulties.*

During the past twenty-five years of family counseling, Gayle and I have found ourselves continuously in awe of the basic happiness of most small children who live in abusive homes. It usually takes years of physical or emotional trauma before this fundamental state is finally destroyed. Live television reports from war zones, refugee camps, and areas of famine often capture the capacity of children to play and be happy in circumstances of unthinkable horror. However, to see the difference between how adults and children approach life, it isn't necessary to look further than a party.

Lisa

In the late 1970s, shortly after Gayle and I met Jerry Jampolsky—the child psychiatrist who founded the Center for Attitudinal Healing—he invited us to attend the Center's first Christmas party. It wasn't possible for Gayle to make the trip to Tiburon at that time, so I was alone when I entered the long room where all the children were gathered.

I was shocked by what I saw. Before me were kids in wheelchairs and on crutches, kids with muscular dystrophy and Hodgkin's disease, kids with amputated or paralyzed limbs, and kids bald from chemotherapy. As I looked around this room of horrors, I sensed that something was out of place. Although there were children of all ages present, most of them were 'tweens and teens, and as you might see at any party, they were gathering in groups of twos and threes, talking to each other. There was no entertainment as yet and the food had not been served, but as my eyes went from one child to the next, I realized that just as I would expect "healthy" children to be, these afflicted kids were happy. The "something" out of place was their attitude. The room was filled with their giggling and laughter.

Soon I found myself talking to a teenage girl named Lisa,

who had worked very hard the last few years to perfect her skills as a model. Now half her body, including her face, was paralyzed from a car accident, and she was standing by means of aluminum crutches that clamped above her elbows. As two other adults and I talked to her, she suddenly lost her balance and fell straight backward, hitting the floor like a tree. When we got her to her feet, there were tears in her eyes from the pain. But Lisa smiled a crooked smile and said, "At least I'm finally getting a hard butt."

"Getting a hard butt" is not spiritual language. But what could be more spiritual than this girl's reaction? I have no idea what Lisa's religious beliefs were. Nor do I know if any child in that room believed in God. But the light, the laughter, and the joy of the Divine poured from them all. They needed no belief for that to happen, but they did need to be in the present, as children so often are. What was especially instructive to me was that their healed minds were more real and important to them than the wreckage of their bodies.

To replicate a childlike approach to happiness is not to behave as children behave, but to see as they see. It is letting go of narrow perceptions and habitual responses. It is relaxing and restfully acknowledging that the people around us are the way they are and that we are here with them. To "become like a little child" is merely to relinquish our need to judge all things, change all things, and be right on all occasions. This removes the blocks we put on our capacity to enjoy, or at least to be still and at peace.

> There are only three things you need to let go of: judging, controlling, and being right. Release these three and you will have the whole mind and twinkly heart of a child.

If nothing else, little children are direct. They feel what they feel; they know what they want. Clearly, they are connected to their cores, their basic natures. But children are not perfect and invulnerable. Actually they are more vulnerable than most parents seem to realize. They take on both the positive and negative lessons that their parents and early life experiences teach. They especially pick up the strong unspoken fears and urges of the adults around them.

You may look back now and remember that as a small child you could see that a certain approach to life on the part of one or both of your parents was a mistake. You may even remember thinking that you were not going to make that mistake when you were grown. Yet, as an adult, perhaps you have found yourself saying the very words or acting the same way you were determined to avoid. You took on a pattern even though you were aware it was a mistake! That's how vulnerable we are as children. As adults, we can become more conscious of the taking on and letting go process and thus take charge of the peace and well being of our minds.

Perhaps you know a child who has become judgmental and controlling at much too young an age. I'm not speaking of "the terrible twos," because a close look at this stage shows that although it's filled with lots of "No"s and "I won't"s, there is really no bitterness or deep grievance behind any of this. The child is simply trying out "taking the wheel"—a good and necessary stage.

Yet there are children who learn judgment, even hatred, at a surprisingly young age. The need to control always comes along with censure and self-righteousness. You don't like what you see out there and you want to change it. In fact, you believe it's your moral duty to change it.

If you have seen this happen to children, you know that they also lose contact with their basic happiness and certainty. They have been taught to doubt others and they can't help but apply that lesson to themselves. Once they begin doubting themselves, they think they must control themselves. They are not reliable, and, naturally, no one else is either.

When our minds are given over to judging and being right, individuals of any age think they know how they want the world to look. But now their attention is riveted on what is outside of them. To "look in their hearts" becomes a strange, even frightening concept. It has been so long since they cast their gaze in that direction that they doubt that anything but darkness is there.

Letting Go of the Fear of Letting Go

Letting go of judgment and control has no downside. What possible harm could come from practicing the simplicity of not having to be somebody, and of not requiring our friends and family to be other than who they are? We can cross the street without becoming a "pedestrian." We can drive to work without becoming a "commuter." We can walk the dog without becoming a "pet owner." And we can extend our hand to our child without becoming "the parent."

We only need to be as we were created—effortless, present, and free. No additional history, status, or attitude is required. What need have we to make money, education, religion, or race the banner of our righteousness? What need have we to stand apart from one another, wrapped in our childhood damage like a bloody cloak? Our childhood is over. All our accumulated differences are like dust on the skin, and the members of our human family hold out their hearts to us each day.

If we could dine out without turning into the "customer," we would have a chance of feeling our equality with the person serving us. If we could report for jury duty without turning into the "citizen" who must deal with a "county clerk," we would have a chance of seeing our oneness with the person who stands before us. Our identity can change like the distorted reflections in a line of storefront windows—or it can remain the same, like the lovely image of a child held forever in the heart of a parent.

> *Those in our lives who make the most meaningful and enduring contributions to who we are have dared to take their place among equals. The world stares in amazement at the glittering adornments of the ego, but only those who walk beside us in love and equality reach our hearts and transform us.*

release 1

Suggested time: 1 or more days

The next time you are in a store, restaurant, mall, workplace, or just walking down a crowded sidewalk, pick out one or, if you have time, two or three individuals, and, in turn, practice becoming them for a few moments. How does it feel to wear their clothes (can you feel the cloth against your skin?), to have their hair or no hair, to walk as they walk or cannot walk, to gesture as they gesture? Do their eyes occasionally look to the side or dart around like all of our eyes do, as if the one inside who is looking out is a little uncertain, a little vulnerable? It's a very big, unpredictable world out there. Without analysis, inferiority, condescension, or perspective—

in other words, without thinking about it—what is it like to feel as they feel and think as they think?

Try doing this today, and if it is enjoyable, for the next few days. Perhaps you will be struck with ordinariness. Perhaps you will sense that we are pretty much alike, and that we are all in this together. And perhaps you will feel a little sad for the occasional person you see who tries so hard to stand rigidly apart, only to find loneliness and isolation.

Letting Go of Mental Pollutants

Cleansing the body of toxins and releasing the muscles of tension are familiar procedures in holistic medicine. The need for physical purification is so obvious that, as a concept, it has become a dominant goal in self-treatment practices and within conventional medicine as well.

For example, many brand-name vitamins and nutritional supplements found in chain drugstores now are advertised as purifying and cleansing agents. Within alternative healing circles, numerous cleansing procedures such as fasting, high-fiber and raw-food diets, enemas and high colonics, saltwater baths, and numerous "therapies" such as heat, breath, Vitamin C, and water are recommended and trusted. Within the body-mind-spirit movement, everything from exorcisms to the burning of sage is used to cleanse rooms, residences, and buildings of their negative forces.

In the mornings, we shower and brush our teeth. During the day we wash our hands after each visit to the restroom. We use special antibacterial products to cleanse "kitchen surfaces." Our laundry detergents include disinfectants. Our dishwashers super-heat the water. Many homes and even some cars now have air filtering systems. Tap water is out and purified water is in. A growing number of people carry liquid "hand sanitizers" to cleanse their hands of germs after coming out of a store or restaurant.

It's curious that we are so preoccupied with cleansing our bodies and environment of everything that can harm our health, beauty, and energy, yet we feel no real need to cleanse our minds of what can sour our attitudes, block our intuition, tear apart our relationships, and undermine the very aim and purpose of our lives. Yet what do those who are physically pristine gain if within their sparkling habitats they live in a downward spiral of darkness and misery? What difference does it make if a body is always scrubbed, detoxified, and all its surfaces germ-free if no living thing the body encounters is comforted?

In our houses of worship, we pay lip service to the truth that our bodies are mortal but our internal spirit is everlasting. We sing hymns and listen to words that denounce the outward and corruptible and praise the inner and eternal. We even say that time will end and the world will pass away but that "within us" is the kingdom of heaven.

Yet in daily life, we obviously are not concerned in the least about what is within. All we care about is getting the outside clean. Each day we walk forth with clean clothes, clean hair, clean teeth, but with a mind stuffed with worthless anxieties, dull resentments, stale outlooks, toxic prejudices, and an endless array of shabby self-images. We haven't even bothered to sweep out the mental junk we picked up yesterday, not to speak of the debris we have been hauling around for a lifetime.

Our mind is not some little unencumbered spirit free to

traverse whatever airy realm it chooses. But we would like to believe it is. We see movies and read books about fantastic fantasies and unfettered thoughts. We talk to children about the "power of the imagination." We attend seminars that tell us our minds have immense reserves of untapped capacity. All in all, we have done a superb job of kidding ourselves that in our roomy "attic" all is useful, worth keeping, and in good repair. But if we observe our minds closely for just one hour, we see that instead of a boundless chamber of magic and wonder, our minds are more like stuffed and stodgy refrigerators that emit peculiar odors. Pick any shelf and just one brief expedition reveals items in the back so old we don't even remember acquiring them.

Nor have these containers of leftovers and ancient jars of condiments been sitting quietly in the corners where they were pushed. They are now so thick with mold and mildew that they have taken on lives of their own. Indeed, the back recesses of our refrigerator mind are in revolt and have set up sour and stinky kingdoms of their own. It's so scary a sight that our impulse is to shove all the front-line items quickly back in place so that now sunny orange juice, freshly picked mangoes, and organic celery once again appear to be all that's in there.

It's not a small task to clean out our overstuffed minds. It takes a little time and courage, and we have to brace ourselves for some unpleasant discoveries. But when the shelves are once again clean and orderly, when only fresh edibles and true nourishment are on the horizon, and when soft aromas fill the air, we will know we have made a very small sacrifice for such bounty.

> *This book asks you to swim against the tide of opinion: Decide that happiness is an essential part of a life well lived.*

It's curious that I or anyone would have to make a pitch for simple peace and fulfillment. Yet this illustrates the state of modern culture. It is acceptable, if not expected, that individuals devote huge chunks of their lifetimes to accumulation, professional status, physical attractiveness, social acceptance, and a better golf swing. Mention enjoyment and inner ease and most people think these are luxuries they don't have time to pursue. It's enough to hope that their life might someday look successful.

If you want to know what it feels like to stock your refrigerator with the items you choose rather than those chosen for you by culture and family dynamics, just look at little children playing—which they do most of the time. The average preschool child laughs over 350 times a day. The average adult laughs about ten. Why? Because children come into the world with clean refrigerators!

So let's begin. To help us assess how much mental litter we collect in a single day, let's consider just one useless item that we all accumulate: worry.

Letting Go of Worry

Very few people are convinced that worry is useless mental debris. Somehow, it just seems right to worry. We reason that since everyone does it, it must serve a purpose. This is like saying that since we all betray each other in little ways, betrayal must be beneficial to the human species. It is patently untrue that each human impulse has a positive aspect and fits into "the grand scheme of things."

> *To progress spiritually, we have to acknowledge that we make mistakes, sometimes bad mistakes, and that we have at least some innate tendencies that are harmful and unreasonable.*

"The wisdom of the body" is highly questionable, as anyone with insomnia or allergies is reminded almost daily. The wisdom of the brain, as part of the body, is equally questionable. In fact, the body, including the brain, doesn't react consistently or as a whole to anything. What is good for one part of the body is often bad for another part. In countless small and large ways, the body divides and wars against itself and is often the primary cause of its own destruction.

Likewise, the mind has many parts, each with its own agenda. For instance, it often longs for something and is repulsed by it simultaneously—whether money, sweets, sex, or leisure. We simply can't say that because most minds worry, they do so "for a reason." Not every human proclivity is rational, as is shown for example by the staggering number of humans who must be confined to jails, penitentiaries, psychiatric wards, and mental hospitals throughout the world. So let's first examine several "enabling" attitudes our culture has about worrying to see if there is any benefit in using our minds in this way.

Seven Attitudes That Enable the Worrier

Attitude 1:"It's natural to worry."
Every day we construct a shrine of worry and carefully set in place each cherished object of concern. There is often a central focal point of worship—perhaps an upcoming event or a question about our health. The subject may seem reasonable, yet notice that an embarrassment from the day before or even from ten years earlier can also occupy an honored place at the shrine. It's as if our aim is to worship problems, not solutions; to worship questions, not answers. We are quick to find fault with any remedy that comes to mind or that someone suggests, just so we can keep worrying.

But isn't this "natural"?

Certainly it's natural in the sense that it's universal. But so are tooth decay, death, jealousy, colds, accidents, losing one's train of thought, hiccups, arriving late, forgetting names, and lecturing teenagers. Very few of us would argue that these natural states and traits are beneficial. Worrying doesn't cause us to feel more comfortable or facilitate better decisions.

Worrying fragments the mind, shatters focus, distorts perspective, and destroys inner ease. Worrying is self-afflicted distress. It has no consistent practical outcome, one that can be predicted and relied on. For example, worrying is not planning. Indeed, worry can delay and even prevent the planning that would otherwise remove a chronic concern. Worry is mental chaos and feels bad. Therefore it is junk—but junk we accumulate and endure every day of our lives.

release 2

Suggested time: 1 or more days

One day is all you need to prove to yourself the effectiveness of this Release, but it's a tool you can use to great effect for the rest of your life. This Release also illustrates several of the fundamental concepts of this book, namely, that our ego is our desire to be separate; that the experience of connection or unity with someone or some thing outside ourselves neutralizes our ego; and that sincerity (focus, commitment) is the key to successfully letting go of anything.

• Identify a line of thought that is torturing you.

This should be a piece of cake. You probably already have one in mind. Perhaps the two most common ones are something we keep worrying about, and someone we keep arguing with in our mind. The first involves the future—a fear of what might happen. The second involves the past—distress over someone's behavior or distress over the way some event played out.

It's important to see that even if what we can't stop thinking about is an event, other people's reactions are central to our distress. Our mind doesn't get stuck on events that no one else witnesses or will ever know about. If for instance we do something really stupid while hiking, we may laugh about it, but we don't keep going over and over the mistake—unless of course we know that the mistake will be obvious when we return.

The reason I make this point is that our ego is always up to the same thing—to create more separation (more difference, distance, or distinction) between ourselves and others.

- The next time you notice the line of thought you have identified, interrupt it (just don't complete it).
- Then think of something, anything, that contains love or connection.

Think of your dog. Think of your garden. Or your partner, child, friend, or a loving relative. Or think of God or the light of God. Or perhaps think of a scene of thoughtfulness, generosity, forgiveness, or humor between two people—an event you once witnessed or were involved in.

To bless, pray for, or hold in light the person who is the object of your worry or judgment is also a connecting thought and a very powerful one. However, you may not be able to do this if your feelings about this person are too disturbed, in which case any other thought of oneness or joining will do.

Just identify the thought. Interrupt the thought. And think of anything with love in it. Do this procedure even once and you will see that you can always let go of a distressing line of thought in the present. Most people, however, don't seem to know that.

We believe that we simply can't stop worrying or judging—it's just something the mind does—so we halfheartedly fight this mental activity by getting mad at ourselves or by trying to reinterpret the situation.

The mind-splitting effect of getting mad at ourselves is perhaps obvious. Yet many people assume that reinterpreting what someone did or what some future event will mean is a gentler, more reasonable approach. Actually, the effect is the same. We introduce a new interpretation to do battle with our first interpretation and thus split our mind. We never quite believe the new interpretation ("He probably wasn't trying to hurt my feelings; he just gets yelled at a lot at work"; "She probably wasn't trying to cheat me; she's just scared her store isn't going to make it"), and our minds go back and forth trying to decide which way to look at it.

Meanwhile, the anxious or judgmental line of thought continues, and, eventually, we give up and resort to just enduring the distress, hoping it will soon run its course. In this way we spend hours or days in an unhappy frame of mind.

Even then it's not over. As soon as one thing we are concerned about or smoldering over is finished, another upset takes its place. This dynamic is one of a thousand reasons that learning to let go is fundamental to our happiness and peace of mind.

Once you prove to yourself that any distressing line of thought can be released in the present, the problem then becomes that three minutes, an hour, or a day from now, the thought comes back.

Where does it come from?

Any thought that distresses us is a product of our polluted, conflicted mind, which from time to time I will also refer to as "the ego." The ego part of us wants to distinguish itself from other people. Its goal is to be set apart, different, and unequal, and it correctly sees connection as its mortal enemy. Worry thoughts and attack thoughts create a sense of isolation. The longer we pursue them, the more cut off we feel, thereby fulfilling the aim of our ego.

Therefore, to permanently let go of a distressing line of thought, we must set a goal of connection and mental wholeness and make that more important than our ego goal of separation.

- Plan out what your response will be the next time your ego offers you the line of thought.

You want the response you set in place to be very brief and direct. You will interrupt the thought and you will . . . surround in light the person about whom you have been having revenge fantasies. Or say to yourself, "I put the future in God's hands." Or think about how funny the new kitten is. Or picture divine light filling and cleansing your mind.

Once again, any thought that is in some way loving, happy, or peaceful is sufficient, because it contains connection, and your ego does not want you focusing on connection.

- Decide to be sincere. Say to yourself, "No matter how many times my ego brings up this thought, I will respond as I have planned. I will out-endure my ego. If it brings this up a thousand times, I will respond one thousand and one times."

Once your ego sees that, for example, you are going to hold the person in light whenever it suggests that you think of her or him in a distancing or separating way, it will stop bringing up this line of thought. Perhaps it will test your sincerity a few more times, but this particular form of distress will fade away surprisingly quickly once you take a permanent stand.

The procedure I have outlined for stopping a distressing line of thought does work as neatly and consistently as I have implied. Yet I want you to know that I often have trouble applying it. This is not because it's in any way a complex or tiring procedure, but because I am conflicted about actually giving up the line of thought.

Whether the thought is one of worry or judgment, all distressing thoughts come from our desire to be separate, to be right, to stand apart, and so on. This desire is stronger in us than our desire to be whole, connected, and at peace; otherwise, these struggles would never arise in the first place. When I see that I am not consistently applying the above steps—identify the thought; interrupt the thought; think of a subject of connection; put in place a plan for when the thought returns—I have found that I save time if I take a moment to consciously realize that I do indeed want to stop using my mind to torture myself, shatter my peace, and put myself in a mental position where I am of no use to those I love. Above all, I must become clear that I want to look upon the people involved in the line of thought with gentleness and understanding rather than with censure. This may not be easy if I am angry with them. It always boils down to the question I can only answer for myself: Do I in fact want to walk toward God, toward Love, or, through justification and judgment, away from God?

Attitude 2: Failure to worry is risky, if not dangerous.
The general assumption is that if you are "a happy camper" today, tomorrow "the other shoe will drop." "Happy-go-lucky" is the same as "devil-may-care"—and we all know what happens to those who don't worry (care) about the devil. The word *happy* itself is sometimes used as a substitute for "reckless," "crazy," or "lacking good sense," as in "slap-happy," "power happy," "divorce-happy." Many children were raised hearing this cautionary theme in stories such as the parable of the silly grasshopper who enjoyed summer versus the wise ant who spent summer collecting food for winter (then had the self-righteous pleasure of refusing to help the starving grasshopper!).

Furthermore, we all grew up seeing—and more importantly, feeling—our moms and dads worry about their weight, the weather, insurance, bank balances, and a hundred other concerns. Most school-age kids, having parents who are too careless or insensitive to shield them from their fights, and who already know many kids with step- or single parents, worry about whether their own parents are going to divorce. This can become a particularly deep-rooted and debilitating worry because it relates to safety, self-esteem, and survival. For this and many other reasons, most of us begin our adult years with the basic fear that nothing is reliable, not even our home.

Not only is worrying fanned through parental insensitivity, most parents aggressively teach their children that they should and must worry—about how much or little they eat, about catching an endless list of diseases, about whether they can trust their own basic nature or common sense ("I can't let you out of my sight," "You don't care about anyone but yourself"), and about "too much junk food," "certain people," bad grades, and on and on.

Moreover, as children we were given grounds for a basic all-pervasive worry through every "Are you sure?" question we were asked:

"Are you sure that's the water gun you want to buy? This green one will last longer."

"Are you sure you want to invite Ian to your birthday party? Remember, he didn't invite you to his."

"Are you sure you don't need to study for the parts-of-a-flower test? You don't want to end up pumping gas for a living."

"Are you sure he/she's the right one for you, dear? You don't want to start dating again after you've lost your looks."

Even though our propensity to worry comes primarily from our childhood interactions with our parents, other sources contribute mightily. The underlying sense that it's good to worry is part of our overall culture. In the West, we join together daily to hear endless reports of problems with no thought of seeking solutions ourselves. Drinking in the problems is satisfying enough, and the media knows it.

Religion, which should foster comfort and healing, can promote worry, if not terror. Ministers, priests, and rabbis often use fear to sell doctrine and increase contributions. Even many twelve-step groups try to motivate through fear.

Clearly, our educational system fosters anxiety as well. Our schools set impossible goals, all the while dispensing "consequences" for a bewildering array of "inappropriate" behaviors. Grades K through 12 have multiple and, in many ways, conflicting aims: responsibility, socialization, self-esteem, environmental consciousness, creativity, racial pride, drug awareness, time management, and the like. Homework assignments are constructed to reflect so many different values that most kids don't know what the teacher expects. Teachers themselves vary widely in how they want to influence their kids because the textbooks and curriculums they are handed contain complex and confusing compromises.

Behind all these early lessons from culture, home, church, and school can be heard a drumbeat of conflicting warnings: "Better watch out," "Go slow," "Use your head," "Watch your step," "Watch your back," "Know who your friends are," "Trust no one," "Mind what you're doing," "Look ahead," and, my favorite, "Think twice." Obviously there are ways to use these sayings well, but like today's "spiritual" worries ("Be mindful," "Be aware," "Watch what you're putting out there," "Fears are self-fulfilling," and perhaps the scariest of all, "Remember, you create your own reality"), they contain one underlying message: We are more alert and better armed when we are anxious.

That's absolutely not true. The opposite of a worried mind is not a foolish mind, but a still mind. The simple, observable fact is that a worried mind is busy, cluttered, and scattered, whereas a still mind is more capable of broad, steady awareness, if for no other reason than it is less distracted. A worried mind provides no protection. A still mind can assess the surrounding situation more quickly and accurately than a mind dominated by anxiety and thus is less likely to overlook a present danger.

Attitude 3: Worries are intuitive or predictive.
Obviously, an anxious driver will drive more safely than a depressed or indolent driver. But simply because under some circumstances one kind of mental junk compares favorably to another kind doesn't mean that both are not junk. A driver

with a cold will drive more safely than one with advanced pneumonia, yet in either case there are better physical states to be in when you drive.

In this book, we are looking at what cleanses the mind, focuses it, and makes it whole versus what fragments it and robs it of peace and presence. The belief that you should put up with an agitated mind simply because there might be an accompanying premonition that could come true is just plain silly.

It's true that a thread of intuition is occasionally mixed in with a worry, but there is no reliable way to tell whether intuition is present this time. For instance, many adults make parental decisions based on worry. Look at the mixed results. Gayle and I are a case in point. As a child, Gayle was forced to make her bed daily, whereas I never was. Today, I like making beds and Gayle doesn't. As a child, I was forced to hold in my stomach but Gayle never was. Today Gayle does not have the resistance to waist-trimming exercises that I do.

Out of worry, most parents come down hard on a particular behavior because of their fear of how their kid might turn out. Much of the time, this brand of discipline is enduringly destructive—even though occasionally a dire prediction will come true. We tend to ignore the vast number of predictions that fail.

> *If the goal is to discover what state of mind is most intuitive, worry has to be eliminated on the grounds of inconsistency alone.*

Because enough people have noticed the idea that fears are not intuitive, even this insight has been turned into a worry. Have you heard the saying, "It's the things you don't worry about that get you"? Taking this literally means the more things you worry about, the more you eliminate from getting you!

Unfortunately, the chaos of the world will see to it that some of the things you worry about do happen. As another saying puts it, "Just because you have a phobia of flying doesn't mean the plane won't crash." Worry is a no-win game.

 release 3

Suggested time: 1 day

Our fear that what we said to a friend yesterday might have been misunderstood would have no meaning and be of no interest to us if we knew for sure that the person could carry no memory of our remarks into the future. If this were the case, we would know that the friendship would remain unaffected despite our comments. Our fear therefore is not about what we said, but about future ramifications. When doing the second Release, keep in mind that although they have their roots in the past, all forms of fear point to the future.

- From the time you awake to the time you get ready for bed, write down any fear that crosses your mind. Include every worry, vague apprehension, nagging suspicion, or catastrophic fantasy you notice.

- Before you fall asleep, mark those fears you most strongly believe will come true, or if you prefer, rate each fear on a scale of one to ten; ten being absolute certainty. In other words, single out the fears you think are intuitive and predictive, as well as those you suspect are self-fulfilling because of the intensity or frequency with which you think of them.

- Post this list where you can check it from time to time. In the weeks and months to come, see for yourself if anything happens the way you imagined it would. Also, take note of all events that conflict with what you feared, events that in some way turn out to be the opposite of what you worried would happen.

- When most or all of the fears have had sufficient time to occur, fold the list and put it in your purse or wallet. This will be your new identity card. You are now a person who is not afraid of fear. If your ego steals your card, you can renew it simply by repeating this one-day Release.

- Should you choose not to do this Release even once, you must renounce forever your right to worry out loud.

Attitude 4: There is a time and place to worry.
When our car skids out of control or when we trip and fall, our mind is usually surprisingly calm. Only afterward do we get stirred up and start "sweating" the accident. What good would it do to worry about our options, about possible physical consequences, or about what lesson "the universe" is trying to teach us while we are twisting in mid-air to lessen the effects of a fall or struggling to regain control of a car? If we used our mind to worry during an emergency, we would introduce conflict and hesitation into our reactions. We would be unable to respond instantly. Does this mean that worrying might be useful when we are not in an emergency?

Younger Brother

When we were in our late teens, my brother and I were invited to visit a ranch in the mountains of Colorado. One day when we were hiking, we came across a magnificent waterfall almost two hundred feet high. I dared my brother to climb it with me and he accepted the challenge.

Our plan was to climb beside the flow of water, and although we didn't have climbing equipment, the grade seemed mild enough that we didn't think we needed it. As often happens with inexperienced climbers, what doesn't seem steep from below seems impossibly steep once you are on the slope. By the time I saw that this was turning out to be more difficult and dangerous than I had guessed, I realized that it would be even more dangerous to attempt to climb back down.

We were about thirty to forty feet from the top, just below a huge rock outcropping, when it started to hail. Soon the hail turned to rain. I could see no way to the top from my side of the outcropping; ordinarily I would have circled around to my brother's side, but suddenly the shale we were standing on began loosening.

Being the oldest of the two and the one who had made the dare, I was in the lead. As our footing began to wash out from under us, I became worried. The longer I stood there thinking of the disastrous consequence each option before me could bring, the more my muscles tensed up. My brother chose that moment to tell me that he had heard that climbers had died attempting to scale this fall on two occasions. Hearing that, I froze completely. I literally could not move an inch.

Despite my frozen state, I could still talk. I assured my brother that from where I was standing, I could see a way to the top from his side of the outcropping. This was a lie but it was the only thing I could think of that might get us off what was slowly becoming an avalanche. Fortunately, my guess turned out to be right, and when he climbed to the top, he reached down and helped me up.

A natural reaction to this story would be to say that I worried at the wrong time. If I had worried before we started to climb, maybe we wouldn't have gotten ourselves into danger. Clearly a rule such as "Worry before but not during" won't work. That rule would have made me question accepting the invitation to visit the ranch, question the thought of taking a hike in unfamiliar terrain, and so on. Often it isn't even clear what point is the beginning.

When is the right time to worry? Our plan could have been to climb part way up the falls just to see what the view was like. If that had been the thought, should we have applied the rule "before but not during"? Actually, there were several points along the way when it still would have been safe to go back. Should we have worried about finding and acknowledging the exact no-turning-back point? If we agreed that this point had been reached (people seldom agree when to stop), should we have paused and worried then? During the climb, we saw a snake that neither of us had seen before and we inched closer to get a good look. Should we have worried before we started the inching or at the point we stopped to look?

Obviously there is no formula for the right time to worry. Perhaps it could be said that "a little worry" is a good thing. Perhaps it's the amount and not the time that's important. Maybe if I had worried a little we wouldn't have ended up in life-threatening circumstances. Yet the fact that the climb looked worrisome made the thought of doing it exciting. Who would dare someone to climb a wide, gentle slope covered with a thick cushion of grass? If we hadn't been "a little worried," the climb wouldn't have been a challenge. It seems that I needed to worry more than I did, but how much more? Obviously I worried "too much" when I stood below the outcropping.

The thought that there is an exact amount of worry needed is just something more to worry about. Once again, no formula exists that will indicate the degree of worry needed. The fact is worry begets worry; and neither its time nor degree can be controlled, nor can its effects be foreseen. Worry doesn't work.

Attitude 5: Worrying is a sign of intelligence.

We think that worrying is an intelligent choice made by the individual as opposed to a mass reaction to a collective mind-set. Yet worry is the uniting emotion of the world. It can make allies of any groups or individuals. It cuts across religious, political, racial, and sexual differences. News and magazine-format television programs have mass appeal because the viewer can count on a steady diet of new things to worry about. "Investigative reporting" reveals dangers in places we never suspected. Anxiety produces chemical changes that the body grows used to, and addiction to anxiety in its various manifestations is perhaps the most common of all addictions.

Many people think that the question, "What's the worst that can happen?" is a useful line of thought that brings them a certain objectivity and keeps them from overreacting. In our culture, a person free of worry is considered naive. We think that cynicism is a sign of intelligence and practicality. Since disaster overtakes us all, we tend to view peace of mind as an unrealistic or dishonest emotion. Don't all things end, and surprisingly quickly? The strong prey upon the weak until they too are weak and are preyed upon. Everything we see lives off the death of something else.

The conclusion is inescapable. You and I will wither and die like all things, whether planet, person, or plant. The best that can be said about how it all turned out for us personally is that as we died, we suffered less than others. This, then, is the background scenery that only those in denial can keep from noticing. Therefore, we assume that worry is the "aware" emotion, the one that is induced by the facts.

Our choice is simple. We can focus on the "inevitable" facts of life, or we can focus on where we are and what we are doing. When we relax within the situation at hand, whatever it may be, we begin opening up to another reality that our pre-composed picture of the future can't show us. Awareness of this reality eventually brings us the experience of the Divine. Worry is always about the future, even if the future is the next moment. Worry blocks awareness of the Divine because the Divine is now. The name of God is "I AM," not "I WILL BE." Remaining unconscious of God is not an act of intelligence.

Attitude 6: Worrying is a sign of compassion.
We also think that those who worry are more empathetic and socially responsible. We believe that our angst demonstrates our concern that so many people in the world are suffering. Does worrying connect us to these people? Does it heal anyone? Because anxiety is somewhat unpleasant and tiring, a false sense of accomplishment can ensue. A bout of worrying often gives us the sense that we have done our part, when in fact we have merely spun our mental wheels, or our mouth.

Notice how cut off you feel when you are around someone who is apprehensive. Individuals who worry are, at least for the moment, self-absorbed. The subject of their line of thought may be someone else, but they don't extend love to that person. "I'm worried for you" is typical of the ego's self-canceling approach to life.

Thanksgiving dinner is often an example of this use of worry. These meals typically begin with a prayer that includes words such as, "Let us remember all those who are starving." If we were actually to do this, if with each bite we thought of a starving child or a hungry nation, we would eat in enormous conflict. There could be no experience of joining and oneness at such a table. Those gathered there would not feel more connected, more loving, or more generous toward anyone, nor would those who are starving be any better off. Generosity is an act of happiness, not an outgrowth of fear.

No day passes that we don't see before us some reminder of an old or new misfortune that came upon someone unexpectedly. The media loves to spotlight those who have fallen victim, especially to the new danger that the article or program is trumpeting. It's almost unthinkable that we would remain free of fear after hearing and seeing, day after day, the thousands of tragedies that occur to people just like us. Simply because that is the effect doesn't mean that worry is a useful state of mind. Worry is a fear state, and fear is tentative and uncommitted. It causes our mind to withdraw, turn in on itself, and shrink. As the Bible and other sacred scriptures point out, the strong unifying force of Love has within it no aspect of fear.

Attitude 7: When things go well, you'd better start worrying.
If a book or movie begins with happy scenes and cheery voices, we know something bad is about to happen. In every life a little sunshine must fall—but not for long. Notice that the very fact that things start going our way spurs us to worry.

From sore experience we learn that what we desire most can hurt us most. Many athletes are unable to live up to the expectations generated by a huge contract. Books tell the tragic stories of lottery winners, rock stars, movie stars, and other celebrities. Tabloid news shows and tabloid newspapers are filled with the devastating effects of power, wealth, and fame on individuals who attain them. Oddly enough, many of the fairy-tales and children's stories that were read to us for enjoyment recount the ironic outcomes of granted wishes.

Even in everyday conversation people say, "Be careful what you ask for—you just might get it." Think of the implications of this statement: The special advantages with which you might start your life—good looks, good immune system, natural talent, inherited wealth, or something else—are untrustworthy. Yet the extras you hope and pray for are even more untrustworthy!

Our problem is not that we don't look danger and irony in the face. We stare trance-like at the world's threatening visage. What we do not question is the value of this way of looking, the actual benefit to us of a worried perception.

Letting Go of Our First Reaction

These seven enabling attitudes are not particularly difficult to see through, and most of us eventually begin to recognize that worry decreases our ability to adjust and react; to be creative, intuitive, and sensitive; and certainly to know simple enjoyment and peace. Nevertheless, most people believe they have little control over their mind's tendency to fret and brood. Have you seen the bumper sticker, "If You're Not Worried, You're Not Paying Attention"? In other words, awareness must lead to worry. Most of us suspect that worrying is innate, part of the very nature of our mind. Through concentration and force of will, we may combat the magnitude and volume of worry, but we will never eliminate it. Anxiety is like some suffocating national religion and, like it or not, we too must kneel before the shrine of worry.

To a limited extent, this perception is realistic, and the goal of a worry-free mind is unrealistic. Yet if it's true that we will always worry some, it must also be true that inner stillness and peace are unattainable. At any moment, worry, being more elemental and powerful, can interrupt stillness, however deep that stillness is.

The Psalmist writes, "Be still and know that I am God." Perhaps you have seen someone you love experience this kind of stillness: A mother holding an infant. A man after surviving a heart attack. A child quietly watching a kitten play. My guess is that you too have been "at peace" at least once, if not many times, in your life. Perhaps when you least expected it, the wings of peace enfolded you and you knew that nothing was real compared to this state of simplicity and rest.

I mention these states that some call "the peace of God" to show that, unquestionably, worry can be stilled. However, a religious, spiritual, or transformational experience is not the only way to quiet worry. A shift of focus is actually all that's required. However, before we examine the minor shifts that eliminate minor worries, let's examine how the mind accomplishes this during times of great need. Strangely enough, extreme examples often are very helpful in clarifying the approach that is most serviceable in everyday circumstances.

If your child has just been diagnosed with a life-threatening illness and no one can tell you the outcome, you will not only worry, you will agonize over what might happen. Don't believe for an instant there are normal people who can receive news about the possible destruction of their own body or the body of a loved one without having an emotional reaction. It is recorded in more than one holy scripture that saints, prophets, and even God "weeps" over the pain experienced by ordinary people.

During times of tragedy, what is not helpful is a new concept or belief, even if it is spiritual. Yet so many people today think this is all it takes. Ram Dass has often told a story that illustrates why concepts don't work. It's about a guru who counseled a woman who was grieving over the death of her son that she should not be sad, because within the Divine there is no death. Years later, the guru's son died and the woman, seeing the deep grief of the guru, reminded him of what he had told her. "That was your son," answered the guru. "This is my son."

Naturally, when faced with tragedy, we are going to worry, grieve, be outraged, and react in all the ways normal people react. This book would merely place an additional burden on anyone reading it if it suggested that humans should not react as humans. Our first reaction need not be questioned, but eventually we can and must ask if that is the only response of which we are capable.

Returning to the example of receiving news about our child's illness, there comes a point when we question whether continuing to use our mind to worry benefits us, our sick child, or anyone. We never have to remain locked in our first reaction. Whatever the tragedy, ultimately we want a mind that brings us peace, and we want a mind that extends peace to others.

Some friends of ours and their daughter provided us and many others who know them with an uplifting example of this.

Tom and Ann

Two years ago, Ann and Tom's twenty-one-year-old daughter, Diana, had a seizure and they took her to the emergency room. Subsequent tests indicated a brain tumor, and thus began a nightmare of getting second opinions, taking time off from work, arranging for Diana's absence from college, deciding on a hospital and surgeon, and all the other problems involved in a crisis like this.

Neither Gayle nor I have interviewed Tom and Ann's daughter, so this story is told from a parental point of view. As parents of three boys, we have experienced more than once what it is like to have a child in grave danger. So, not only because they were friends but also because they were loving and deeply spiritual parents, we were keenly interested in what they faced and how they handled it.

Tom is a doctor and Ann assists him in his practice, and they told me that at first all they could think of was finding a cure for the tumor. However, after a few days of approaching their daughter in this way, they decided to reexamine their purpose. In part, this shift came from the realization that their panic and terror were making Diana's ordeal more difficult. As a result of what they called "prayerful examination of our hearts," they decided to love Diana "with every fiber in our being" and to devote themselves entirely to her peace and happiness.

Although they took all steps necessary to have their daughter properly diagnosed and treated, including traveling out of state to get the best medical help, their focus was no longer Diana's physical recovery. They knew that numerous outcomes were possible, including death, various degrees of incapacitation, or complete recovery. They told me that in their life they had noticed that some people can turn to God only when they are very sick and some only when they are dying. They also said they had known individuals who had expressed thanks for their disabilities because of all they had learned from the experience. To put it another way, Ann and Tom understood that they were not in a position to judge which exact physical outcome was in their daughter's best interests, and even if they were, they couldn't control events.

Let me say here that this state of mind is very difficult to explain to anyone who has not experienced it. It can sound like not caring whether the person recovers or trying only halfheartedly to see that the person does recover. Therefore, some readers might be surprised that Tom and Ann were fierce advocates for their daughter's care and treatment. They did not hesitate to confront nurses or doctors if they thought their daughter was being neglected or a mistake was being made.

Yet how could this be if their purpose now was to make their daughter's happiness more important than her physical recovery? Because fighting for her recovery was the appropriate expression of their love for her and of their desire for her peace. Recovery was extremely important to Diana and to them. That was an inescapable fact. Any normal mother and father would care deeply whether their child recovered from a brain tumor. Fighting for Diana's recovery symbolized their love more powerfully than any other possible action. That did not mean that their heart's goal and the focus of their thoughts was changing her body. To the contrary, it was bringing comfort to her spirit.

> *Declining to make control our aim does not mean that we perform the tasks and duties before us sloppily or halfheartedly. If our purpose is awareness, all things must be done attentively. If our purpose is wholeness, all things must be done meticulously. If our purpose is to love, all things must be done with care and beauty.*

Ann and Tom's purpose of loving their child and bringing peace to her would also have allowed for the possibility of stopping their advocacy of medical treatment, if at some point their daughter had simply been through all she could take and wanted to die. Gayle and I have seen far too many people focus on a particular physical outcome to the exclusion of what was best for their loved one—whether spouse, child, or elderly parent.

You should know that despite Tom and Ann's good intentions, the situation was so terrifying to them in the beginning that all they could do was try to see their daughter lovingly instead of fearfully and to act comfortingly around her. However, as they concentrated on Diana's happiness, they gradually began to experience their oneness with her and soon felt a deep peace that carried them all through the weeks of tests and a long operation.

The operation was a success and Diana is now back in college and once again participating in sports. This outcome was not inevitable. Ann and Tom understood that "God, who loves us all equally, did not single out our daughter for a brain tumor or to be one of the few who fully recovers."

Letting Go of Motivation through Crisis

If you've had anxious people hovering around you, perhaps it's clear why Tom and Ann's shift in focus would make Diana happier and more relaxed. For most people in our culture, it is not clear why this shift would make such a profound difference to Tom and Ann. Simply put, it transformed their minds from garbage dumps to gardens.

If more of us could experience what it is like to go through just one day with an unfragmented, unconflicted mind, a day in which we react to all things from our own wholeness, a day in which we see other people clearly because we ourselves are clear, a day in which we are truly and deeply ourselves, there would be no need for motivational seminars, inspirational sermons, or self-help books. We would already know reality; we would have experienced it firsthand. Now we are like children pointing and screaming at a shadow, while all the time a loving parent stands behind us offering us safety and support. That parent is the comforting presence of stillness already in your heart. When the mind is unified, there is nothing to block the quiet beauty of the heart.

Many people can muster the resolve to weather a storm, but the cumulative effect of ordinary events overwhelms them. Tom told me that after Diana returned to college, the peace he had felt began to fade. When he noticed this, he started to pray more often to get it back. To his surprise, this did not work. The reason quickly became clear: now his priority was to give to himself alone.

Even when you pray, if you pray without love or connection, you may have a temporary sense of peace but you will not touch the eternal peace within your heart. There is no kindness in first thinking of yourself, then trying to be kind to yourself alone. Love is not an act of isolation, and "loving yourself first" is not a step toward happiness. You will never satisfactorily nurture just your own wounds or your own needs, because those concepts include no unity. Only what joins us to another can heal us and make us happy.

The reason Tom lost his peace was not because it was no longer necessary to spend extra time and money on his daughter. We extend ourselves to others by bringing them into our hearts, not by making dramatic overtures and spending lots of time. Certainly we can extend peace to another while doing a good deed—in fact, good deeds often help open our hearts—but an empty gesture, no matter how spiritual it looks, can also make someone feel a lot worse.

> First love; then do what you do. First choose peace; then say what you say. Asking, "What should I do?" "What should I say?" really means,

"How do I get the outcome I want?" "How do I control this person?" Seldom are we confused if we make peace and mental wholeness our goal.

When Tom saw his mistake, he began devoting himself more to his wife, his staff, and his patients, especially in his thoughts and prayers. He told me recently, "Whenever I give to the people around me with the singleness of purpose I gave to Diana, I just feel better   I work better; I enjoy my patients more; Ann and I are closer; and life is worthwhile now. It's simply in our best interests to be kind."

If we look at the process that allowed Tom and Ann to refocus their minds and release their worry, anguish, and fear, we see that they shifted their attention from a outcome they could not control (finding a cure for the brain tumor) to one they could control (loving their daughter and seeking her peace). Whenever our sincere desire is to improve our own state of mind, we cannot fail. What we usually do, though, is try to improve our state of mind and control some aspect of the situation. This fails because we have split our mind.

Ann and Tom did not try to force their daughter to look or act peaceful. They weren't seeking a pretty picture. They were offering their comfort and peace in every way they knew how, but Diana could easily have resisted this. Gayle and I have seen many sick and dying people close themselves off and become unreachable, and that is their right. Such a choice never prevents the people around those individuals from silently blessing them, even if from a distance, if distance is what the sick or dying person wishes.

release 4

Suggested time: 1 or more days

- Today, pick two or three small errands or tasks—putting on your clothes for the day, going into a convenience store, fixing a simple meal, paying a few bills, or some other short activity.

- Before you start each activity, take a moment to settle your thoughts and become inwardly still. If you don't have a usual way of doing this, perhaps you might try quietly repeating the words, "All released. All is peace."

- When you feel that you are as peaceful as possible, set the goal of making no conscious decisions or choices during this one activity. Each time the sentence layer of your mind cranks up and begins trying to decide anything ("Should I wear these shoes or those shoes?" "Should I pay with cash or credit card?" "Should I fix soup or a sandwich?"), interrupt the thought, quiet your mind, and just do something, anything. But do it with as much stillness and peace as you can.

- After the activity, take a little test. First, ask yourself if you believe the quality, efficiency, or wisdom of anything you did during that activity was impaired by your having gently declined to decide.

If the answer is no, review the activity again. This time ask yourself if you believe you acted more smoothly, efficiently, and wisely than you would have if you had made conscious choices in the usual way. (Yes, these are loaded questions.)

Letting Go of Emotion Fixation

S ince the 1960s, popular and professional psychology has targeted the emotions of individuals as if they were a kind of control panel for mental health. Media has increasingly leaned toward emotion-driven stories—if the president gets mad, for instance, that in itself is a story. Talk shows—both radio and TV—now solicit and provoke expressions of feelings from their guests (as opposed to expressions of ideals or beliefs), and an amazing array of support groups and twelve-step spin-off groups have sprung up, centering on the emotions of their members as the primary agent of change.

Not only have we come to think of emotions as the key to mental health and the primary agent for changing behavior, in the last few decades emotions have become the gold and jewels of our culture. In the 1950s, the acceptance speeches for awards and prizes often centered on where the ribbon or plaque would be hung and how the honor conferred would affect the recipient's future. The books on public speaking frequently recommended that the speaker compliment the appearance of the trophy or award. Today, on the other hand, it is widely accepted that the true reward is in how we feel—as is the true loss.

The question sure to be asked about anyone's public tragedy is how has this made the victim feel. The post-event interview with the winner of any contest now always begins with, "How do you feel?" Days later, the follow-up question is, "Has it sunk in yet?" (The answer is always "No.")

Mid-century athletes with a quiet, workmanlike affect were admired. In those days, for a woman to be called "sweet" or a man to be called "the silent type" was a compliment. Today's athletes are expected to pump themselves up and play with intensity. Adults, and now teenagers, who are quiet are suspect. To be called "the silent type" today means you may be psychotic.

So commanding is the new role assigned to emotions that "the feeling is gone" is a frequently cited justification for having an affair or divorcing one's life partner, and is often the unspoken justification for changing one's religion or kicking one's teenager out of the house.

> *"How do you feel about that?" is one of the most regularly asked questions in support, therapy, and twelve-step spin-off groups. This question makes the person's feelings about what was said more important than what was said.*

None of this is to say that awareness of emotions is unimportant. Emotions are a language that speak to us of the deeper workings of our mind and if listened to—rather than reacted to—can provide valuable insights into our selves, our children, loved ones, and friends. Yet, in themselves, emotions are not a proper destination point. They are a door that must be seen but also must be opened.

Behind every emotion is a thought. We think our friend might die and we experience fear. We think we are being slighted and experience anger. We think we are being misunderstood and experience frustration. A thought generates each of these feelings. Emotions don't arrive from nowhere. They fall and rise on the waves of our thoughts.

Because emotions are by-products of thinking, we sabotage our careers, health, happiness, and relationships through unconscious thinking, not unconscious feeling. This is why learning to recognize a polluting thought the instant it shows itself is crucial.

Most people have a general awareness that they are sad, irritated, anxious, or discontent—just some of the emotions symptomatic of polluting thoughts. Yet surprisingly few people take time to identify the thoughts behind their emotions. Individuals may be critical of themselves for how they are feeling, or, more likely, blame someone else, but most of us don't uncover the mental contribution we ourselves make. This is like being vaguely aware that something is "off" or "out of sorts" in the body, but not focusing on what or where it is.

As a culture we have come up with many ways of dealing with our emotions and especially our emotional outbursts. Some of these ways are effective; others are destructive. Blaming, drinking, "venting," overeating, retaliation (now called "justice" or "closure"), confrontation, entertainment, vacations and "respites," sexual release, support groups, prescription drugs, and music all can at least change, if not improve, our emotional state. But they can't change it permanently. We have settled for the fix without going for the cure. We have many painkillers for the pain, but the broken limbs remain broken.

What is actually broken is our mind. This is why, when it comes to emotions, nothing works for very long. Notice that the same person, event, comment, or circumstance can strike you one way at one time and any number of other ways at other times. If you think back to your childhood, you will remember that this was one of the confusing, and perhaps scary, aspects of your parents', teachers', or coaches' reactions. You didn't know what to expect. They were always over-reacting or under-reacting to what you said or did, and there was no real way to figure out what they wanted from you this time. Their mood was out of your control because it was out of their control.

A few nights ago, Gayle was at a large department store sale and saw a mom pulling her five-year-old daughter behind her from one display table to another. "Hurry up!" the mother barked. "Can't you see what I'm trying to do here!"

"But Mommy," Gayle heard the little girl say, "I'm being as good as I know how to be."

The tragedy is that that scene—especially when coupled with interoffice feuds, varying intensities of road rage, and the long fuse of disagreements burning within most "love" relationships—is the rule rather than the exception. Just like this mother, we have lost our understanding of how to enjoy life and have put in its place a relentless churning of our own and each other's emotions. Inner turmoil is unquestionably distracting and addicting, but is mere intensity the primary experience we want from life?

Letting Go of Money Anxiety and Travel Worries

In the last chapter, we used the example of a child's grave illness to show how a shift in focus can replace the emotions of anguish, panic, and worry with mental stillness and peace. Even when dealing with lesser emotions such as anxiety, nervousness, and apprehension, the approach needed to let these feelings go operates the same way. For instance, I travel with some frequency, and as the time approaches for me to leave town, I invariably start to worry. I have learned to interrupt the worry by asking myself what my purpose is for going.

Let's say I have been invited to give a workshop. My worries tend to be about whether I will make my plane connections; whether I have packed everything I need; whether I will get enough sleep; what kind of group will attend the talk; and other factors beyond my control. The simple fact is that I have never taken this trip and cannot foresee what will occur. Even that realization doesn't stop the worry.

What does stop it is focusing on what I plan to bring mentally to each aspect of the trip. That alone is under my control. So how do I want to pack? In peace. How do I want to say goodbye? Lovingly, sincerely, and in the present. How do I want to wait in the airport? With relaxation and enjoyment. How do I want to treat the people I encounter? Kindly. What kind of workshop do I want to give? The most helpful one I can. And so on. Focusing on what I can control unifies my mind and dissipates fear, because only a fragmented mind can produce fear and other disrupting emotions.

Money concerns are another example of a usually less-than-tragic problem that many of us face. If I assume that you are the one who pays the bills; juggles credit card interest rates or debt; sets aside savings if you can; and invests if and when money is left over, then I'm sure you are well aware that each of these tasks is unpredictable and riddled with pitfalls. For instance, did all the bills come in? Are all the charges accurate? If a creditor needs to be put off, how will that creditor react? Can you count on the mail delivering your payments on time? Will the economy make your investment a wise choice? And on and on. Of course you are going to worry, but is worry all you are going to do?

Certainly if there are children involved, deciding money questions by putting your kids' interests foremost is an excellent way to switch from a fragmented and worried mind to a focused and united mind. Even here, there is no way to know the best financial choice. There is, however, a way to know what you believe is the best financial choice. Asking yourself what your love for your child dictates can be a simple and peaceful way to see what you believe is best.

For many people there is not an obvious person whose interests they can put above their own when making financial decisions, and putting themselves first can get complicated when money is the subject. For example, is it okay to take risks that might lead to greater financial freedom if the risks involve only ourselves? Or perhaps we should become tight-fisted since there is no one out there who can provide a safety net. Or maybe we shouldn't have savings since there is no beloved heir.

Money questions, like all questions, do not require anxiety or confusion. Setting a mental goal and making it more important than present circumstances or future outcomes stills the mind and restores wholeness. It's perhaps easier to understand making the peace and well-being of our partner or child our only aim, but the process involved is actually the same. Whether our purpose is to think of loved ones in peace and extend that peace to them, or to think of our finances in peace and extend peace to that area of our life, we still must change our inner focus from worry to peace.

For instance, if paying bills is a particularly anxious time for you, before you start, you might close your eyes and silently repeat, "I will read these statements and write these checks in peace." Continue slowly saying this until you know that your purpose of remaining at peace has been firmly set.

Then, as you pay the bills, any time you start to become anxious, lean back, close your eyes, and reset your goal.

No sound financial decision can be reached through fear and worry, nor do you solve a problem by punishing yourself mentally for mistakes you may have made before. No one knows the "right" investment, or exactly how much to save, or whether a bill can be skipped for another month. Our mind will always fragment when we ask a question that is impossible to answer. When we seek what is already ours—a whole mind born of God and held in God—then our thoughts settle down and our mental process relax. A "state of mind" by definition occurs in the present, and stability is the more natural condition of this state.

> Whatever the question about money is, we can always see which choice we believe to be the most comfortable; which one we think we are least likely to chew on later; which one holds the prospect of the least amount of fear and the most peace. No one can predict what will happen, but questions directed at our own peaceful preference can always be answered—if we are willing to sit quietly and look at our heart's desire.

Letting Go of Anticipated and Unanticipated Emotions

The option to choose a focus that unites the mind is available to us only after the fear first enters. This of course holds true for any disrupting emotion. It will do you no good to oppose the feeling you just became aware of—whether jealousy, discouragement, shame, or worry. In this respect, an emotion-free mind is an unrealistic and unhelpful goal. Notice how difficult it is just to keep from worrying about when it will stop raining or whether we chose the right checkout line at the market. Clearly, there is no magical way to steel our minds against ever starting to worry, doubt, despise, despair, or the like.

Trying to keep ourselves from experiencing a particular emotion in the first place is an even bigger mistake than trying to fight it once we are aware of it. When we attempt to preempt it, we risk hiding the emotion rather than letting it go. Unseen, the thought behind the feeling continues to operate, but with far more power than before.

If a destructive emotion were just a set of physical sensations, then perhaps we could will ourselves to ignore it, like we sometimes will ourselves to ignore a backache or "fight" a cold. But an emotion is the symptom of a thought, and attempting to block the emotion is ignoring the thought that's causing the feeling. Denying a destructive emotion is like denying the symptoms of a cancer or a broken leg. The cause goes untreated and the damage expands.

Unless we uncover our reasons for feeling the way we do, merely battling our tendency to feel that way will do little to free us. Recognizing the actual harm done to ourselves and others by fear, anger, hatred, self-loathing, and other products of mental pollution is a necessary step toward freedom, but there is another equally important step. We must expose the thought that is producing the emotion, and we must expose what we're doing to empower and retain that thought.

If we can clearly see that we don't believe the thought behind a particular emotion, we have the option of replacing it with a more natural, restful, and self-affirming mental activity. If we want to end the vicious cycle of using our minds to torture ourselves, uncovering the thought behind our first wave of emotion is fundamental.

Letting Go of Victim-Perception

The world never strikes us the same way twice. This, of course, is an ancient insight. Shakespeare wrote, "There is nothing either good or bad, but thinking makes it so." Thinking is always changing, which also means emotions can always be changed. At present we are victims of this fact, but it is a neutral fact, and we can use it to great advantage. Ordinary people and ordinary events have surprisingly little effect on our happiness and peace until we add our highly personal interpretation to what just happened. Once we do this, we become victims of our own perceptions and believe that what we ourselves are doing to the world, the world is doing to us.

Shopping Cart Rage

A few weeks ago, as I left the checkout line at a grocery store, I saw two shopping carts, each containing small plastic bags. I assumed that the one nearest me was mine and pushed it to my car. As I picked up the bags, I noticed that their contents were not mine and turned to go back to the store. Just then, an angry-looking woman accompanied by an assistant manager came out of the store and headed in my direction. Pushing my stolen cart, I met them halfway and said to the woman, "I must have..."

"That's my cart!" she yelled.

"I know, I must have..."

"That's my cart!" she yelled again.

Each time I started another sentence, she interrupted with the same three words.

By now I was angry. "Could you say that one more time?" I asked her.

"That's my cart," she answered.

"Thank you," I said. "That's very good."

Not liking that exchange, the woman reached out and jerked the cart out of my hands, even though I had already handed her the bags.

Then I saw that the assistant manager had the cart with my bags in it. Remarkably, he apologized to me, although I'm not quite sure why. I thanked him, took my bags out of the cart, and that was the end of the incident.

In thinking about what had happened, I realized that I had had no particular reaction to her saying "That's my cart" for perhaps ten or fifteen seconds. My anger came when the thought "I don't have to take this" entered my mind. Looking at this thought more closely, I saw it was more accurately, "I am not a person who is obliged to be treated in this manner." Or, "I am not a person to be trifled with." Or, "I will not be disrespected." As you can see, I was now looking at the woman through the lens of my own false dignity and had to come to the rescue of my ego. This one thought made me a victim—because now my pride was vulnerable to her anger. Yet the thought was merely my personal interpretation of what was happening.

Consider all the thoughts I could have had as I stood there: "This is rather funny." "How is the assistant manager reacting to all this?" "I bet I work this into my upcoming sermon." (I did.) "Here is still another example of my absent-mindedness." "What has happened in this woman's life that this is so important to her?" "The sun is shining. It's a beautiful day. And this will be over soon." "What would be my reaction if this was a gorgeous supermodel?" And so on. Each of these thoughts would have generated a different emotion. On the other hand, if the woman had thought of me as a hunk (I realize I'm stretching here), she would have spoken in a different tone—or at least not have felt quite so confident that she could jerk the cart away from me.

release 5

Suggested time: 1 or more days

This Release presents an insight that we will return to several times. Our minds are stuffed with so many thoughts, so many voices from the past, that many of them conflict. Destructive as some of these thoughts are, they do us little harm until we take one of them to heart. Whenever we feel a disturbing emotion, we can be certain that we have made this mistake.

This Release does not deal with the problem of identifying thoughts. It assumes that you already know at least some of the ones you habitually embrace, and so it focuses on the embrace, not the thought.

- Today, identify as many of your distressing thoughts as you can. Write them down. Stick the list in your pocket. And when you find yourself thinking one of these thoughts, reach in your pocket and squeeze that list as hard as you can. Then say to yourself, "The thought itself isn't the problem. Squeezing my mind around the thought is the problem." Then relax your fist. Relax your mind. And look around. There's a lot more out there than what these thoughts are telling you.

Letting Go of Word Magic

Same scene + different thought = different emotion. Here's where many people get off track: They believe they can erase their first thought by saying words that represent another thought. This overlooks an important fact: thoughts are a reflection of what we believe, or at least of what we think we believe, at that moment. Words simply are not a substitute for beliefs.

In order for thoughts to change, our beliefs have to change. Just saying words to ourselves doesn't change our belief; it merely sets up an argument in our mind. Now our mind is split between what we believe and what we are telling ourselves we should believe.

Some people, in a situation like the stolen-cart drama I was in, might say to themselves, "What would Jesus do?" But that's not necessarily what they're thinking. Consequently, part of their mind is going, "What would Jesus say?" But the other part of their mind is really thinking, "I would like to strangle this cart-obsessed woman."

> A friend of mine told me about a woman she knows well who was always saying, "I love my body." "I love my body." "I love my body." One day my friend asked her, "Well, do you love your body?" The woman broke down crying. "No," she said, "I don't love my body." Of course not! Words are not thoughts. Words are just the package that thoughts usually come in.

Once we think a thought—that is, once a belief takes form in our mind as words—that thought becomes the lens through which we see the world. Of all the things out there, this thought determines what we select and what we overlook. In a sense, a thought is a stand, a position, and we comb through the data before us and select what supports our position.

Gayle and I know a man who has the thought, "Hollywood is no damn good." He believes that Hollywood is no damn good. In fact, he is capable of spending an hour or more citing examples to support his belief. Even when we all sit in the same theater, we see a radically different movie than he sees. On the other hand, we have had the experience of liking a particular actor's work, reading something negative about that person, and experiencing quite a different performance the next time we see that actor.

One might say that the article "colored" our view of the actor's performance, but this implies that there is a real performance and a colored performance. If a hundred people sit in a theater, each sees a different performance because their beliefs vary—even though a few vague descriptive phrases might be agreed on by some.

Letting Go of Stories

In counseling parents, Gayle and I run across many moms and dads who don't really see one of their children; they see only the thoughts they have about that child's basic character. These dark thoughts cast a shadow over everything the child does, and all of her words and acts become part of the belief held by the parents.

Unlike movies, books, dreams, and the like—which are representations of reality—children, adults, and other living creatures can be experienced directly. Provided, of course, the mind is quiet. Toward the end of this book, we will examine in more depth the effects of mental stillness. However, so that a misconception does not begin growing from all we have discussed about how thoughts determine our experience of events, please don't entertain the tiniest doubt that truth exists, that God is at hand, and that you and your loved ones are real. It is patently untrue that "everything is a projection."

The interpretations we bring to the images our eyes see are unquestionably a projection. But the light we behold in the heart of our child, the peace we know when we think of our beloved, and the beauty and wholeness we experience when we open our mind to the Divine are unchanging, everlasting, and simply cannot be corrupted by the word-formulating layer of the mind.

The part of us that interprets, judges, and reacts does not even see the eternal. It can't touch truth because it doesn't know truth. Although we all have this busy, fragmented, unhealed part of ourselves, we also have a deeper awareness that is connected to others and united with life, a conscious-ness that already rests in the embrace of Love and beholds the children of Love. The ability to see is already in place. It need only be cherished.

> We have a profound tendency to confuse what we see with how we are looking. Those who remain unconscious of how their thoughts char-acterize themselves and the ones they love sim-ply miss life altogether.

It is vital that we see ourselves, our children, our partners, and other loved ones directly. Otherwise we live inside stories of our family, stories of our friends, and never touch anything real. You may know many couples and individuals whose sto-ries about their marriages, their lives, and their children's lives are more real than the people involved. When you are around these people and see them actually relate to each other, they are like cardboard figures having cardboard exchanges. The actual relationships have in many ways ceased to exist and most of the emotions the people now experience come from the tales they weave about themselves and their relationships. Each new event—a vacation, a promotion, a sickness, an affair—is looked at only in terms of how it will fit into the tale of their lives.

Certainly we all see this happen to many people who become famous. Within a surprisingly short span of time, they cease to exist. They merely become stories. Anyone they know who won't go along with the story is discarded. On a less dramatic scale, this happens to most of us. Our lives drift into unreality, and our old age resembles a wax museum with the same stories narrated in the background over and over.

Please don't let this happen to you and to how you relate to the ones you love.

For most of us, going though a day is like opening a very old coloring book in which the pages are pale and all the outlines of figures are dim. Yet our thoughts are a set of vivid colors that we apply to scene after scene, page after page. Once we realize that the colors we use, not the vague outlines of figures, are what dominate our mind and call forth our feelings, we can begin focusing on what we are creating with our thoughts.

In other words, once we see that our own thoughts coat the events of our day so thickly that in many ways we are reacting to a life found only in our own minds, we can stop looking at, reacting to, or trying to control events and start observing our thoughts.

All Emotions Are Not Equal

Those who pursue a "higher" path and those who strive for an unusual degree of self-discipline are usually trying to think perfectly, feel perfectly, or act perfectly. Very often they also are trying to set themselves apart from "the crowd," or ordinary folk, and consequently they never get past the more obvious ways they vandalize their opportunities for happiness and damage the people in their lives.

Unlike the aim of some therapies and spiritual teachings, in this book we are not attempting to get at the thoughts behind all emotions, just at the ones that wreck our lives. If not released, anger, bitterness, arrogance, or revenge—to name just a few of the more poisonous emotions—can dig a hole deep enough that it might take a lifetime to climb out. Yet momentary feelings of laziness, boredom, or tranquility, although not the peace of God, will cause little harm to anyone.

Even when the effects of the more disrupting emotions are not life-altering, to some extent they always hurt you or the ones you love. The obvious exceptions to this are the temporary angers and judgments stirred up by reading a newspaper letter or editorial, watching a TV report, hearing a story about how the friend of an office acquaintance was treated, and the like. The grievances we take to heart and the dark decisions we make about people close to us can tear apart our families, injure our health, and damage our capacity to enjoy almost everything.

release 1

Suggested time: 2 or more days

- Identify the dominant or most persistent feeling of disturbance you have had in the last few hours, or if you can, in the last few days or weeks. The next time you experience this emotion—fear, hatred, disdain, cynicism, despair, or some other destructive feeling—sit quietly within the emotion and write down every thought you notice, no matter how unrelated it seems.

- Continue sitting with this emotion, recording every thought that crosses your mind, until the emotion begins to change. Then set the list aside for further reference and go about your day as usual.

When you first sit down and begin searching your mind for thoughts, it's not uncommon to find that your mind suddenly goes blank and your primary emotion lessens. If this is the case, just begin writing down any vague impressions of thoughts, moods, or attitudes that you notice. ("I sense a mild anxiety. It seems to be centered on me, possibly on my ability to do this Release. No, it seems broader than that. It seems to have something to do with the way things are going in my life right now. . . .")

If even that much specificity is not possible, begin describing the mental blankness itself. What is this blankness like? ("My mind seems uniform and gray. But I am aware of sounds and sensations around me. The blankness seems to contain a kind of sadness, almost is if the blankness were quietly sobbing. I notice this sobbing vibration in my hands also. Oh, I just had a thought. It was, 'I feel more dejected than I should.' Or maybe, 'I am more dejected than my life circumstances warrant.' Or, 'I am too self-pitying.'—Something like that.")

If you keep watching your mind, very shortly thoughts will appear. The sentence layer of your mind simply can't keep quiet for very long. So be patient; describe what you can; and shortly your problem will become how to write it all down. This too need not concern you, because our minds think in circles, like a merry-go-round. Any thought you overlook will eventually circle back. In future sittings, you will be able to get to the thought content of your mind more and more quickly, and you also will become more relaxed about thoughts you miss as you see them return again and again.

If nothing else, this Release should expose how stuffed our minds are. Notice that most of your mental contents are not even yours. They do not come from your deepest convictions, your intuition, or your experience. Sorting through these bits of memory, fantasy, pronouncements, images, and fears to find the one or two thoughts generating this emotion is like going through the refrigerator looking for what's causing the smell. Sometimes we think, "Ah heck, I'll just clear it all out and start over." Now that's good thinking, but it's a little beyond the first task that must be mastered: becoming fully conscious of what our mind is up to.

Most people attempt total cleansing too soon and end up suppressing many life-impoverishing thoughts that should not be suppressed. If you notice times when you overreact or times when what you just said or did surprise you, some very productive and freeing efforts can still be made.

• Obviously, our minds are capable of many random, off-the-mark thoughts. After at least two thought-recording sessions—perhaps spread over two days— look over your lists of thoughts and put a mark by any you flatly do not believe ("Maybe my cynicism is caused by a new food allergy," "I feel defensive because I have no real complaints about my childhood," "I should interrupt this exercise and call someone about that old, stuffed refrigerator noise," "Suddenly everyone's teeth are white except mine—that's why I'm sad") and disregard these thoughts for now.

- Of the remaining thoughts, at least one or two should stand out as clearly aggressive or destructive, as occurring more frequently within your lists, as defensive, as self-attacking, or as having a "charge" in some other way. (Here are some typical thoughts: "It just never ends," "All men think about is sex," "Women are crazy," "Nothing I do is ever good enough," "Sooner or later they always leave.") Select from your list the thought or thoughts that you believe most likely to be the ones triggering the emotion you are studying in this Release, and write them out in as much detail as you honestly can. We will call these "T-thoughts" ("T" for triggering). They will be discussed further in later chapters.

- In the days to come, every time you recognize either the original emotion or one of the T-thoughts, immediately ask yourself how disconnected or connected you feel to yourself and people around you. If no one else is present, then how distant or close do you feel to anyone who crosses your mind? The answers you get to these questions should begin to alert you to the actual effects on your life that indulging these mental pollutants has had.

- Hang on to all your lists of thoughts and notations.

Letting Go of Misery

Despite the fact that most humans and even most small creatures begin life with basic happiness, frustration is pervasive from the start. It's surprising how much infants cry and how often children of even one, two, or three years of age are distressed and angry. Approaching the world with the directness of a child does not change the nature of the world. The world doesn't work, and children are continually bumping up against this fact. The difference is that children don't stay stuck on the bump. Nor do they make bumps where, for the moment, there are none.

Just look at the people's lives with which you are most familiar. Obviously, few adults can resist the temptation to make crises out of whole cloth. Although infants and little kids get frustrated a lot, whenever there are moments of circumstantial calm, they revert to happiness, whereas adults usually revert to discontent. Why is this? Children's lack of experience creates unnecessary problems for them on many occasions, so adults should have an easier time maneuvering through the world than children.

Letting Go of Neglect

We say that "children have no responsibilities," but a close look at any child's day will show you that kids have just as many important goals as adults. It's just that adults don't take kids' goals seriously. We see a small child get angry at the sky for raining on the very day that his outdoor birthday party was planned, and we laugh because we know that clouds contain no intent and pressure systems can't be controlled. Siblings one or two years older than their sister or brother can't understand why a six-month-old can't be the playmate they were expecting. We laugh when we see them try to get this tiny child to play a board game or to understand the different powers possessed by each action figure.

You would think that the older people become, the more they would learn to take life as it comes. Yet it's almost as if, perversely, we learn the opposite. We not only rail against the sky but against noisy sanitary workers, late checks, botched reservations, people who delay the express line, stores that close ten minutes early, and coworkers who have petrochemicals in their colognes.

As a general rule, humans become more inflexible, fearful, and irritable the older they get. They make friends less easily. They withdraw into fewer activities. Their natural curiosity and enjoyment contract. They become less generous and less forgiving.

Very few people "mellow with age." Although we begin life with basic oneness and good humor, unless we do something to reverse the usual trend, the longer we live, the less connected and more miserable we feel.

This downward slide simply cannot be the result of increased understanding of the nature of the world. The fact is, the more greens you putt, the more you understand how the ball rolls. The more you use a computer program, the better you know its limitations. The more miles you drive, the greater your awareness of how other drivers can behave. Park in front of any high school, and as you watch teenagers drive off, it's obvious that here are people who do not understand how other drivers can behave. Hence a seventeen-year-old is five times more likely to have a wreck than an adult.

If nothing else, age brings experience. So why does it also bring increased stubbornness, ill humor, impatience, and misery? Because we totally neglect our minds. We start out with sparkling new minds, and we do absolutely nothing to keep them that way. In no other area of life—whether our finances, our physical health, or our house and car—do we believe that neglect can have anything but a bad effect.

Let's take as an example the mistakes we make in our relationships. We all do little things, and some big things, to other people that we end up regretting. Every day, relationship mistakes are made in almost everyone's life, yet very few people have a mechanism for correcting these daily. "Too bad," we say, "but these things happen. Maybe I can make it all right with the other person, but usually I can't, in which case the best thing is just to forget it."

There's just one catch. We don't forget it, and they don't either.

If you have had a number of opportunities to talk to people at the end of their lives, you have probably been struck with how many regrets most individuals carry to their graves. Contrary to what most people assume, the regrets of the dying usually are not about the goals they failed to reach, the experiences they never had, or the places they meant to see but never did. Most often their regrets are about the ways they hurt someone or the things they failed to do for certain people. All their lives they have been carrying these heartaches, these very sore places in their minds, and now they think it's too late to heal and be healed.

Without considering the hurtful effects of any other form of mental neglect, just think what failing to let go of this one category—the ways we hurt other people—must have on our spirits, our welcome of the morning, the peace of our sleep, our exuberance and vitality, and our capacity to have fun. Neglecting our minds in just this one way can ruin our lives. This is precisely what happens to most people.

But why would we let it happen? Because we deeply believe that the mind doesn't count.

To the ego, appearances are everything. For instance, the soft part of flannel pajamas is put on the outside—but at least they look soft. The seams of socks and underwear are against the skin—but at least they look smooth. Houses are bought because of their "curb appeal"—but at least they look "very livable." And life mates are chosen because they look good—not because they are good.

Haven't you noticed that good men often don't come in good packages, and that beautiful women sometimes lack inner beauty? As the potential-partner, potential-friend category demonstrates, appearances are decidedly not everything; they are usually meaningless.

Nevertheless, each morning of their lives, most people fail to prepare themselves—mentally and emotionally—for the day. The world over, human beings always manage to get both shoes on, put their clothes on straight, and do something about their hair. It's enough that we look prepared—and this is the key to why we neglect our minds.

Minds can't be seen. They have no appearance value. True,

the effects of people's thoughts can sometimes be seen in their facial expressions, body language, or tone of voice. We usually learn to cover up these effects quite well, and, furthermore, to put in their place bodily signals that make a good appearance. Answering questions such as, "Do you like these shoes I just bought?" or, "Do I look like I've lost weight?" or, "You're sure you're not jealous that my uncle left me all that money?" are moments of concentrated facial and tonal control for most of us. Yet what does it matter as long as it looks like our mind is reacting properly?

Naturally, the solution is not to answer questions like these "honestly." Being verbally literal and hurting people's feelings does not purify our minds. However, from sayings like "Cough it up," "Just spit it out," "Get it off your chest," "Come clean," and even, "Get it out of your system," you would think that hurting through honesty is a form of self-cleansing. Admissions, confessions, and bluntly stated criticisms do in fact shift the burden from the one who speaks to the one who has to hear it, and this does give the confessor momentary relief. Now, however, the person has been hurt once again, and the confessor's burden has actually increased.

Even though telling people how you have betrayed them might seem like "shouldering responsibility" and "making a clean breast of things," it is clearly the opposite. Whether agreeing with a loved one's statement "I'm looking so old" or informing that person that you had an affair, you have failed to be a friend, failed to correct your perceptions, failed to stop acting destructively, failed to handle your own mistakes, and certainly you have failed to purify your mind.

If shifting the burden of our guilty mind onto someone else doesn't cleanse and heal our mind, and if it's obvious that we are not going to forget what we have done, how do we let go of our regrets?

The first step is not to add to them. If our ego is boiling, we must put the lid on it so it won't splash on more people. Otherwise, we draw other egos into the mistake and complicate our situation. When you "vent" on others, notice that now the problem takes on a life of its own and seems out of your hands. If you see that you are about to undercut, criticize, betray, or thwart someone, quickly make a second decision not to act this out. "Do no more harm" is always the first step.

release 7

Suggested time: 1 or more days

* As you rise from sleep, make your purpose only this: "I will go through this one day harmlessly. I will hurt no one in my thoughts or in my actions, including myself."

These are not hollow words. This is a statement of your intent, the goal you now set out to pursue. Returning to this one purpose again and again throughout the day should begin providing strong evidence that the mind does in fact matter and that commitment, although containing no appearance value, has a profound effect on the quality of your life. "I will hurt no one in my thoughts or in my actions" is a purpose that immediately unifies your mind and makes you feel lighter, freer, and happier. Regardless of whether this is noticed by other people, it unquestionably will be noticed by you. If one gentle purpose, sincerely pursued, can have this effect, imagine what it will be like when all your mental garbage has been thrown out and the light hidden beneath the basket of your mind is finally released.

The next step is to question the practicality of indulging in thoughts of guilt, remorse, and regret over the mistakes you have made. These thoughts are a form of self-indulgence. You are failing to take responsibility for your state of mind, because your state of mind is still not being used to heal damage. Look carefully at your thoughts, and you will see that they are all about you and not actually about the one you think you mistreated. This is self-flagellation without sincerity; it is penance without love; it is of no use to you. Guilty and remorseful thoughts do not help, heal, or comfort the person you think you have hurt. In effect, you are simply making the same mistake all over again: you attacked this person; now you are attacking yourself. Attack is the problem, not the answer. The answer is to actively help those you have hurt.

release 8

suggested time: 2 or more days

The success of this Release is strongly tied to your intent. Therefore, continuously check up on your sincerity and repeatedly bring your objective back into focus. Your objective is simple and direct. You want to isolate one mental sore spot at a time and work until you have healed it.

Sticking just with regrets over what you did to another person, or failed to do, bring to mind one instance of this.

A. Review everything that happened in as much detail as possible. Try just to review the facts without taking time to criticize yourself or float off into remorse or shame. If, for example, you didn't attend some event that was very important to another person and you have always regretted this, just go over everything that led up to your not going and everything that happened as a result. Maybe you made an excuse that was accepted and to this day that individual doesn't know that the real reason you didn't go was because you just couldn't be bothered. If so, look honestly at your real motivation. Also, carefully acknowledge all aspects of the emotional price you paid for acting from that motivation.

B. Ask yourself if there is anything overt you can do to make this up to the other person. Continuing with our example: obviously, to call this person now and confess that you just had not cared enough to go would not bring this individual joy or peace. However, if you know for certain that this person is well aware of your insensitivity, then perhaps you could consider sending a very carefully thought-out and complete apology.

When humans apologize, they usually fail to put a period at the end. They add a little explanation. ("I was so self-absorbed in those days," "I was all caught up in my work," "You and I had argued recently." And the like.) Don't fall into this trap. Just apologize. Do a 180-degree grovel and then shut up.

Also, humans often don't make their gestures of apology big enough or wonderful enough. If this apology is truly important, perhaps consider including a really, really nice present. Or deliver the apology in person. Or both. Do whatever you think will more than equal your mistake. Err on the side of overkill. Send people you have hurt anonymous bouquets of flowers. (Anonymity assures that it's sincere.) Send them anonymous gifts of money. (Heaven forbid, did he say money?) Take a vow to say great things about them whenever they come up in conversation. Remember, you are healing your mind, and no effort is too great.

Remember too that when you apologize, the other person will invariably take the opportunity to rehash the grievance, exaggerate the wrong, and, in short, appear to get more angry at you than he or she was before you apologized. Receiving this with grace and defenselessness is part of a real apology. This person needs to tell you what you wouldn't listen to before, so listen now. Do not defend yourself or else your apology will fail to heal your mind.

None of this means that your apology will be accepted. But that isn't your province. Your function is to come to peace with your mistake within your own heart and mind—and there is always a way to do that. Beginning with an overt act, if that is feasible, is good because we all tend to think that outward gestures have more power than inward gestures.

C. If nothing outward can be done—say for instance the person would not welcome any contact with you—then you must make a permanent decision to bless this person whenever she or he crosses your mind. This decision must be sacred. You will always do this, even after this person dies. Once again, we are talking about the healing of your mind, and nothing you do is wasted.

D. If you think your mistake was so great that even this much is not enough to counter the wound you carry, then ask yourself what more can you do.

When my mother died, I was not happy with the way in which I had moved from the town where she lived. Looking back, I realized I didn't try hard enough to explain to her why this move was necessary, and I did not call and write her enough after I moved. Holding her in light, praying for her, and blessing her were not healing this regret. I found I also needed to do penance. I can't describe the penance because it involves someone I would not want to single out. But when I did it, I was healed.

The power of penance is greatly underestimated—not so much penance assigned by another, but penance that comes from our own heart. This heart penance must say, "After I have done all I can to make up for the harm I did you, I will do this one thing more. I will give to my loved ones or to my community or to the world a gift in your name." It will include all that is needed—whether time, money, or service—to say, "I love you; I bless you; I make you whole." And in so doing I make myself whole.

E. The last step is to set in place a plan for how you will deal with regret thoughts that your ego will try to hand you in the future. If you know that you have let go of this incident as best you can, respond in a quick, decisive way whenever any thought of your guilt crosses your mind. Here are a few of many possible responses:

See God's holy presence blessing the entire scene that has come to mind.

Simply say words of truth that remind you that God is near; God understands; and God is leading each of us home.

Briefly hold in light anyone contained in the thought of guilt, including yourself.

Bless each figure in the memory with one brief statement of truth such as, "God loves you and blesses you forever and forever."

> F. Having completed your healing work on one regret, choose another and proceed in the same way. Naturally, the number of hours or days it takes each individual will vary. I'm assuming that you have enough regrets for at least two days' work, but leaving no regret unhealed is your goal and one of the greatest gifts of freedom you could ever give yourself.

Letting Go of Fear of Happiness

We have been using regret as one example of how neglecting our minds establishes misery in our lives. Naturally, we do this in many other ways, but before we explore them it might be good to examine our resistance to exploring them. Adults have a deeply rooted fear, if not terror, of happiness. This is not obvious to most people, but it must become obvious or else making progress toward a whole and free mind is greatly hampered. Perhaps if we look at a few of the more conscious and accessible reasons we choose complexity over simplicity, rigidity over flexibility, unhappiness over happiness, this will become more apparent.

Eight Justifications for Misery

1. It isn't fitting to be happy.

By the images that pour from our TV, by accounts in newspapers and magazines, by the verbal pictures presented on radio and in office conversations, and by the scenes that crowd our memories and fill our dreams, we are continuously reminded that misery and misfortune are normal components of human life.

From all parts of the world—even from within the circles of the most famous and powerful humans on Earth—stories of turmoil and tragedy come to us in an unbroken stream. Little wonder we believe that we have no personal right to be happy. Most of the great spiritual figures throughout history—those presumably closest to God—suffered enormously. In the back of our minds is the dark rumination that if this happens to the least and to the greatest, it's only fitting that it happen to us.

As long as we see circumstances, and not the peace and stillness of our minds, as the vehicle of happiness, we must conclude that any circumstances that favor us do so unfairly.

2. The present is perilous.

Since the future holds bad news for everyone, the present would seem to be all we have left—a moment or two before the inevitable happens. Surely, if there is a harmless way to be happy in the present, it is morally and emotionally acceptable. Surely we respect each other's right to relief when relief is possible.

Although we give each other the "inalienable right" to pursue happiness, we don't give anyone the right to actually find it. As a culture, we simply don't trust people who are chipper now. We suspect that behind every sunny disposition is a sinister motive. It's all right for people to talk about when they were once happy, or to express their hope that one day they will be happy, but it's not acceptable for them to be happy in the present.

We call cheerful people "sweet" or "simple" and dismiss them as intellectual lightweights. We react the same way to happy books, happy movies, and happy philosophies. The reason is obvious. Our own past experience with the present doesn't warrant optimism. Not only is it unlikely to hold happiness, it's likely to be grim. The times most people remember being fully engaged or fully present were when they were extremely sick, or suddenly injured, or overwhelmed with a devastating emotion.

What does the present offer anyone anyway? Even an award received in the present would have no meaning if the next day everyone carried on exactly as they had been. The thought of what will come of it gives the award its meaning. Happiness, then, is experienced most often as anticipation, whereas pain is usually the agent that brings us into the present.

Our minds are usually so noisy that very few people hear the hush of stillness and feel the presence of peace that allows us to experience the living present and timeless now. Only that experience displaces our fear of just stopping and being where we are.

*3. The very circumstances guaranteed to make you happy
add to your burdens.*

In the course of a lifetime, many people get a sufficient taste of one or more of the world's traditional rewards to see for themselves that these cherished windfalls and attainments merely complicate their lives. In fact, the more highly thought-of the prize is, the more chaos, limitation, and misery it usually causes.

Take money for instance. You would think that if someone suddenly became wealthy, they would say, "At last my money problems are over. That's one area I don't need to worry about." But what actually happens? If you think for a moment of the people you know who have the most money, unless you are acquainted with some very unusual folks, they are more preoccupied with money than those you know with ordinary means. They often are less generous with people in service positions, with kids during Halloween, with the jobless, the homeless, and with schools that need bond money. They tend to get more upset than most people with ordinary annoyances such as delays, mechanical breakdowns, bad service, spills, spots, and smells. They often are more paranoid and suspicious of other people's motives. They tend to feel superior to others and confine themselves to a remarkably small number of friends, establishments, and activities.

Physical beauty is another example of what most humans long for that usually ends up hurting them. When the physical changes wrought by adolescence, plastic surgery, a long diet, or months at the spa are over, and now the individual is undeniably gorgeous, you would think he or she would say, "Now I'm so good-looking I don't have to worry about my looks any more." But just sit in a mall and ask yourself which of the individuals walking past are the most self-conscious—the physically beautiful or the physically ordinary? Which individuals entering a restaurant look around to see whether they are being watched? Which individuals attract the most superficial relationships, endlessly worry about their clothes, war ceaselessly with the aging process, and are the quickest to judge others by their looks?

Another universal fantasy is to have many impressive possessions. Yet so unhappy is the subject of owning more than other people that many families break apart in bitterness when property is divided. People who can afford anything tend to stuff their homes and lives with things they don't want and can't use. For example, many of us think we want an ostentatious car—one that is far more costly to repair, far more likely to be stolen, and always must be parked where it won't get scratched; a car that makes onlookers dislike you and merchants charge you more. Owning a vast estate—one that requires endless upkeep—is another common fantasy. Owning several of these, each a great distance from the other, multiplies the problems and number of egos that must be dealt with.

4. A "good catch" isn't good.

Even though they last longer and are more maintenance-free, relationships with a simple man or woman are not as sought after as highly charged relationships with complex individuals. Expectations are immediately lowered if a potential blind date is described as "nice." Individuals who attain prominence often leave those who understand and truly love them and seek instead a "trophy spouse," someone with exceptional bells and whistles. Unfortunately, you have to watch yourself around a trophy spouse. You can't walk around with bad breath and your stomach sticking out. You have to wake up looking good and go to bed looking even better.

Surely the quality sack time makes up for this. Contrary to the notion most people entertain, sex with a stunning partner does not increase physical pleasure. It increases tension and self-consciousness. People who are comfortable with each other and are ordinary and normal in each other's eyes tend to have the most satisfying sex lives. Furthermore, as your looks and worldly importance begin to slip, unless you redouble your efforts to remain worthy, you will be left sooner rather than later by a hunk or a sex symbol.

5. Happiness in moderation doesn't work.

Happiness is untrustworthy even within the much-trumpeted "little pleasures of life." Consider just a few of the most valued categories. The more tempting the food, the more erotic the pleasure, the longer the vacation, the more enticing the betrayal, the more intense the infatuation, the greater the downside. According to one report, every known lottery winner has gained weight, and 85 percent of the men who have died having sex were not having it with their wives. Most of our "moments" have such counter-balancing consequences that eventually we begin to avoid them. Revealing a delicious confidence, criticizing our partner behind his or her back, yelling at another driver, eating and sleeping all we want, or having an "innocent" flirtation can be fun for awhile, but the regret or fear these choices immediately engender and the chaos they eventually bring make them questionable policy.

6. Happiness is "ducking our responsibility."
We believe that happiness is not a serious or important mental state. In this way we sustain our suspicion of happiness by excluding it from our sense of duty. Duty requires that we have our "game face" on. We assume that to take time out to be happy is to put off what we should be feeling. Thus most people have a mild sense of guilt after an episode of happiness. We believe that enjoying ourselves is a not-so-subtle way of avoiding responsibility. Since there is so much in the world that needs to be done and so many wrongs that need to be made right, "taking time out" to be happy seems like turning our backs on the world.

Consider the fact that at least a fourth of the world's population is starving, and always has been. A third of the nations are at war, and always have been. In our country alone, more kids are killed by firearms than all natural causes combined; every twenty seconds a woman is battered in her own home; and 500 adults and children are raped each day.

The number of serious problems facing the world is so overwhelming that it is literally incomprehensible. To single out a few more, there is nuclear proliferation; the erosion of privacy; the threat of economic catastrophe; teenage pregnancies; environmental pollution; mutating viruses and bacteria; political corruption; drug and food poisoning; the spread of terrorism; automobile, domestic, and industrial accidents; the unremitting stream of geological catastrophes; drug abuse; homelessness; sanctioned torture; race, age, and sex discrimination; the mounting extinction of plant and animal species; not to mention the destruction of the planet.

Recognizing the density of the minefield all members of the human family must walk through daily, instead of happy, we should be . . . what? Outraged? Sad? Shocked? Terrified? Cynical? Desperate?

We rarely question the attitudes we are supposed to have in place of happiness. Few ask what comfort and healing, what change for the better, shock, outrage, or the like, bring to anyone? Some say they are the great motivating emotions. If that is the case, then the question should be which best motivates us to be truly helpful—a peaceful heart or an outraged heart? Angry saviors have a questionable history. I would rather be in the gentler hands of Gandhi, the Buddha, Jesus, or Mother Teresa. They got a lot done without anger.

7. Letting go of misery is failing to "honor yourself."

The inner distress we call misery is an emotion or, perhaps more accurately, a cluster of emotions. It is inner pain—the feelings of anguish, fear, depression, sadness, and many other contributing emotions. Yet as distasteful as these feelings are, the internal shift that could give us relief is precluded by the philosophy of our time.

As the primary indicator of our "true feelings," emotions have become our new inner self, taking the place once occupied by the soul, the spirit, or the conscience. Now to question our anger, infatuation, sadness, and many other emotions is to question what is most sacred about us. It not only seems dishonest to let go of misery; it seems like a betrayal of who we really are.

This redefinition of our core has thrown us deeper into chaos, especially since we have also redefined integrity, which used to mean being faithful to our core. Now when we tell someone, "I need to be true to myself," that means, "I need to betray you by following my emotions."

Look at the dilemma we have gotten ourselves into by deciding that our emotions are our truest self. How can we be ourself if our self is changing every few minutes, as emotions invariably do? Not only are feelings never constant, we have layers of feelings heading in different directions. If during an argument we were really to describe all the conflicted emotions we were having about the subject, we would never finish a sentence—because all of it would change even as we described it.

Let's say I have just started lecturing my partner on "how I feel," and I'm on a nice roll when suddenly I realize that I don't feel that way anymore. Now who am I? Here I was in the middle of "honoring myself" when my self abruptly switched. So what should I do? For the sake of honor and consistency, I must persist in making my point—even though my heart is no longer in it.

Since most emotions last only two to three minutes, almost anyone who has had a protracted argument can remember how conflicted they became about what they were saying. The problem is that we are trying to defend an old emotion that is no longer there and are overlooking several new emotions we now sense.

Emotions are like layers of files seen on a computer screen. The one we notice is merely the one we have clicked on. Even that analogy is an oversimplification because the contents of the files have lives of their own and the mouse likes to do a little extra browsing on its own. The bottom line is that if you make your emotions your inner self, you have chaos at your core.

> There is a place within us where we can touch the changeless and beautiful, a place where our real self is experienced in peace. This self does not have to be periodically vented, defragmented, or even defined. In gentleness and ease it is clearly seen, and everything about it is familiar—because this self is consistently whole.

8. Happy people are suspect.

Recently I was standing next to a young tennis pro watching a twelve-year-old girl play a practice match. Although she was holding her own against a more experienced and talented player, she was so distraught with her level of play that she was almost in tears. The pro, still in college himself, said to me, "Her problem is she thinks she should be happy. She hasn't yet learned that happiness is an occasional good meal and, if you're lucky, a good TV program now and then."

That was an apt description of the surprisingly limited role happiness plays in most adults' lives. I suggest that the primary reason its role is so small is that happiness itself is suspect. Just last week Gayle and I were in a mall and saw a little girl, probably about three, walking with her parents. She was completely happy and singing at the top of her lungs. But her mother was leaning down and saying between clenched teeth, "That's not appropriate behavior!"

Of course her mother was right. Under most circumstances within adult society, pure happiness is inappropriate. In fact, people who are too happy too often are considered a little off, perhaps even dangerous. Not only do they get strange looks, they may be passed over for promotion or pulled over for a breath test. It's all right to be quietly pleased when a friend has a setback, loudly pleased when the other team loses, and even to feel fulfilled when you "pay back" someone who slighted you, but if for no good reason you are so happy walking through a mall that you break out in song, you'll probably be questioned by security.

release 9

(This Release is entirely optional. It is designed to reinforce and deepen what we have already covered. If you feel confident that you have a sound grasp of how to identify the thoughts generating your moments of distress or conflict, continue on to "Taking in T-Thoughts.")

A. For the next two days, select at least two times during the day when you know for certain that you are experiencing or have just experienced a feeling of conflict, upset, or distress. Immediately freeze the contents of your mind and carefully search through the thoughts that are present. Your only purpose is to see each thought clearly.

Write a short notation of each thought—the subject of the thought should suffice—on paper you carry with you. A pocket audio recorder can also be used.

B. At the end of each day, flesh out your overall survey of thoughts for that day. Try to uncover any vague or partially hidden thoughts that were behind the feeling of conflict, upset, or distress you were considering. As an aid to seeing these, you might ask yourself the following questions:

- What person or situation appears to be causing or at the center of this emotion?
- What does this person or situation symbolize to me? In other words, what do they represent or remind me of?

Say, for instance, you notice that one or more of your feelings of distress revolved around intrusive sounds—a noisy snack eater at work; a telephone or doorbell ringing at "the wrong time"; a question or request spoken during your favorite show; dogs barking; children screaming. Perhaps you first think of these noises as rude or impolite. Yet in thinking about this a little more, maybe you remember as a child frequently being told to be quiet, or not to interrupt, or never to use your "outdoor voice" inside. Thus your written part might be to say that these intrusive noises symbolize people's lack of acknowledgment and consideration of you and perhaps even their desire to control you.

Another example might be that you see that your feelings of distress or upset come when something of yours is lost or broken. In trying to think what this symbolizes, maybe you remember the disregard your last partner had for giving you phone messages, or passing on gossip that he or she picked up in a conversation, or misplacing the mail, or losing keys. In considering this further, maybe you remember that the things you collected in your room as a child were often thrown away, or your favorite toys were sometimes given to other kids, or one day your pet Guinea pig disappeared and you were told that it had run away. Therefore you might put in writing that when someone loses or breaks something of yours, this symbolizes that you are not being clearly seen or deeply understood.

- What do I believe that makes these circumstances important enough to be upset?

Using the first example above, maybe you would write down, "My capacity to concentrate on what I want to concentrate on, or to continue doing what I have set out to do, or to have my time and activities honored make intrusive sounds important enough to me that I get upset when they occur.

For the second example you might write, "My possessions are important to me. Some carry many memories. Some play a part in ongoing relationships. Therefore when someone loses or breaks something of mine, I feel attacked."

- If I imagine this situation deteriorating or this person's behavior getting worse, what specifically do I see happening to me?

This question entails taking whatever occurred and imagining it occurring more and more often—more and more things are lost or broken; noise episodes increase. As you imagine this, what happens to you emotionally, physically, or mentally? Do you see yourself fading away? Do you leave the person doing these things? Do you become sick, depressed, or suicidal?

    C. Do A and B for a minimum of two days. At the end of the last day, read through all the thoughts and notes you have recorded about these upsets. As best you can, read the lists dispassionately, that is, without judging yourself or others.

As you read, see if there are any patterns to your thinking, any core or connecting thoughts behind most of your moments of distress. For example, is there an overall fear of becoming less empowered, "real," or important? Or are there different versions of an overall fear of losing a relationship or of never getting the relationship you want? Or perhaps many of the thoughts entail money. If so, what appears to be your central attitude about money? Be as honest and specific as possible.

Taking in T-Thoughts

In Release 9, you were trying to find the common thought or thoughts behind your periods of distress. Whether you saw any patterns or not, the purpose of the Release was to practice looking for the links that connect your thoughts and emotions. Increasingly, this practice will allow you to identify the source of your thinking at any moment and to distinguish your real thoughts from what I call your "T-thoughts."

Our real thoughts are whole and unconflicted and are the source of our energy, inspiration, and ability to love. They allow us to see ourselves, other people, and situations as they are in the present. They allow us to experience the place where all hearts join. A T-thought is a core belief that we developed at some point in our lives, usually during our formative years, that now stands in the way of our experiencing unity and peace. When something happens during the day to trigger a T-thought, it automatically clicks on, like a tape or a computer program. If we are not aware of its activity, the set of emotions it produces controls our decisions and outlook.

Since T-thoughts differ with each individual, the same circumstances that upset one person do not upset other people, or if they do, they upset them in a different way. For example,

I recently met a man who becomes furious whenever he sees a handicapped person begging for money. This doesn't upset me; yet when I hear a child begging not to be spanked, I can become extremely distressed.

One characteristic of T-thoughts that is very useful to notice is that we have to recommit to them each day. Until we recommit, they remain dormant. Becoming aware of the moment of commitment allows us to see the nature of the thought more clearly.

The upcoming Release focuses on T-thoughts as the deepest, most powerful source of inner distress. Our plan now is to begin noticing why thoughts that produce disrupting emotions—any disrupting emotion—come into the mind when they do. The answer is analogous to eating one kind of food that appears to have no particular effect on the stomach, but has in fact primed the stomach. Later, perhaps even hours later, another kind of food is eaten and suddenly the stomach feels upset. Ordinarily, the second kind of food would cause no upset, but because the stomach was primed, this time it does.

Other analogies are the flash of anger that comes because we are physically tired, or an overreaction to a traffic delay that comes on the heels of several earlier delays. In both cases, the mind is primed to react.

We prime our minds at the start of the day, just after waking. At this time we "download," or take into consciousness, one, sometimes two T-thoughts. These set up almost every mental disturbance we experience for the rest of the day. Being conscious of this automatic morning download allows us to release much of the power these thoughts have. The reason simple awareness has this effect is that the decision to take on a T-thought is also the decision to believe it. Awareness of what we are doing casts doubt on the validity of the thought and thus weakens it. It also sensitizes us to the thought so that we are more alert when it becomes active during the day.

All of this may raise the question, why decide to take on T-thoughts in the first place? Why recommit to something destructive every day? In part, the answer is that we are looking at the very foundation of our individual egos. Remember, your ego is your desire to be distinct and separate from the people around you. Everyone in a world of separation wants separation, at least to some degree. Obviously, if we could not take this on, we would be completely ourselves, completely free, and we would experience only our oneness with everyone.

This indeed is the goal, but most of us simply are not there yet. We still need to look some more at what blocks our wholeness, oneness, and love. We still need to see how and when we choose to hold ourselves back, and one of the clearest opportunities to see this is when we make our daily decision to recommit to our T-thoughts.

release 10

Suggested time: 4 days or more

- At the start of your day, when you first begin to wake from sleep, quickly survey the state of your mind. Notice that for a few seconds at least, your mind is relatively blank. You always have a moment or two before your habitual mindset kicks in. Your exercise is to observe and record your first thoughts of the day, those you have within the first five minutes. If you are rushed for time, identify each thought by its central subject and fill in the remaining details later in the day. However, if time permits, or if you can wake up a few minutes early, describe each thought in detail.

- Also describe the mood that each thought casts over
  your day. It's possible that the first thought or two
  will place no emotional stamp on the day, but if you
  keep monitoring your mind, very shortly you will
  sense that a familiar mood has just set in.

Some people's T-thoughts may not appear to relate to the
day before them, yet it colors the day and sets in place a kind
of collective interpretation of everything that occurs. For
instance, later that day you might notice a familiar anger
toward a certain group or an old judgment toward a particular person. Or you might feel sadness over events long finished. If so, there will be a central thought that accompanies
these emotions, and it first enters your mind at the start of
your day.

The beginning-of-the-day experience that tells you when
you have just plugged into an old interpretation or T-thought
may be that you suddenly seem to "remember" the meaning or
pattern of your life. The following are just a few of hundreds
of "meaning-of-my-life" T-thoughts we have run across in
counseling.

"I always have to do all the work."

"I will never be understood."

"My spouse (or men or women) is the root of my difficulties."

"Nothing works out for me."

"I have a special mission in the world. ("I am more loved
of God," "I know a truth others don't know," "I have been
assigned a prominent role.")

"I will always be alone."

"I live a charmed life." ("Fate is on my side," "I am lucky," "I have good karma," "Things work out for me.")

"If I could only be free." ("They always take away your freedom.")

"I steal everyone's happiness." ("I cause everyone pain.")

"I never have enough time." ("I must get it done now.")

"Because I am superior, my feelings are always appropriate."

As you can see, there are some positive-sounding T-thoughts in the above mix. People who have this kind of core belief often think there is no need to let it go. They may believe that such an outlook makes them special and gives them high self-esteem. Herein lies the difficulty.

If you have known parents who singled out one of their children as a musical genius, athletic "phenom," or even a "straight-A student," you have seen the problems this kind of "acknowledgment" and "appreciation" can cause. There are few words more dreaded by such a child than, "We know you will make us proud." If this happened to you, you remember the pressure it put on you. Every time you failed to meet this "positive" expectation, you knew you had let your family down. Your parents' love and approval seemed conditional, in part because they were known in their circle of friends by this little legend about you they had created, updated, and embellished for so long.

If our own T-thought is "positive," we put ourselves in the same unhappy position that such parents put their children. If, for instance, your T-thought is, "It will all work out," on closer examination you might see that this belief applies primarily to yourself and excludes most of humanity. Anyone who picks up the paper sees that for thousands, if not millions, of people all over the world, things are definitely not working out. They are dying from starvation, wars, earthquakes, genocide, fires, floods, epidemics, and on and on. If you look even closer, you might see that the "it will all work out" T-thought sets you up for an ever-increasing number of disappointments, as one thing after another in your own body and daily life fails to work out.

Any "positive" or "spiritual" thought that sets us apart from others will cut us off from equality, community, and companionship and will invariably make us judgmental of those we think are different.

People with the T-thought "I'm a optimist, a cheerful person; I always have a positive outlook" gradually distance themselves from those around them. The urge to counter negative conversation with positive conversation is prompted by a judgment against those who are speaking negatively. Likewise, the urge to counter our own negative thoughts follows a judgment we have just made against our own mind. Following up on the judgment with positive conversation or positive thoughts requires constant mental gymnastics as we strive to see everything in some upbeat way.

The antidote to cynical thinking is not optimistic thinking, because we are still reacting, still being a victim of what other people say, still being a victim of our own mind, and still imposing an interpretation on events. With a quiet and united mind, we are able to respond from the present with empathy. We are able to see clearly, intuitively, and freely. We acknowledge what is destructive and what is not, but we feel no need to impose our view on other people. We aren't in a battle with their minds or our own.

In considering your own T-thought, remember that the core attitude that you take on every morning is often quite subtle because it's habitual. The experience most people have is that this is just the way life is. They are just seeing things as they are. If, for example, the T-thought is, "Nothing ever works out," not only will the person interpret the events of the day that way but will often do whatever is necessary to assure that things do not work out. We know an artist with this T-thought who does magnificent work for his own collection but when commissioned to do a painting, or when having to paint for an upcoming show, will not spend the same time and care and invariably puts out inferior work that hurts his career.

Putting on your T-thought in the morning is like putting on familiar old clothing that is no longer looked at closely even though it doesn't fit well. That's why it's helpful to begin your mind-searching period as you start to awake, so that you see the difference between a clear mind versus a mind dominated by a certain characterization of reality.

The coming to mind of a T-thought is often accompanied by a shift in energy level. Many people experience a slight loss of energy when they think this thought for the first time each day. However, if your life circumstances are particularly

exciting at the moment, you may feel an increase in energy
or a generalized anxiety.

Learning to identify the thoughts associated with the day's
first moods, energy shifts, and emotions is particularly useful
within the overall purpose of this book. Therefore, be especially careful to record any thought that precedes a shift in
feelings or accompanies a pervasive mood. By simply recording all the thoughts you have for the first five minutes of your
day, you will soon capture your T-thoughts.

- Although the observation period at the start of
  your day encompasses all thoughts, for the remainder
  of the day simply monitor your mind to see if one or
  two thoughts from the morning continue to appear.
  You may have to work backward in order to catch
  these. First, notice a familiar mood, then search
  your mind for the line of thinking behind it. It's not
  necessary to record these; simply observe them for
  a few seconds, then release your mind to think in its
  usual way.

Release 10 is an important exercise and it would be best to do
it in its entirety for a minimum of four days.

Please remember that it will not help you achieve your
goal of a unified and detoxified mind to decide that you are
selfish, vindictive, petty, arrogant, weak, overly anxious, and
the like simply because you uncover certain thoughts containing these characteristics. There is an important difference
between uncovering thoughts you already have and organiz-
ing these thoughts into a dark, permanent decision about
yourself.

Whenever you become preoccupied with the implications
of any fragmenting thought, this will have a negative impact on
your sense of well-being, your relationships, and your overall

enjoyment of life. Therefore, it's fine to notice the effects of your thoughts on yourself and others, but don't draw conclusions about the basic nature of your heart or spirit. For instance, noticing that you worry a lot is different than characterizing yourself as an anxious person or a person without backbone.

Having said that, you should understand that if you do the work suggested in this book, you will go through a stage of seeing your ego honestly and not liking it. This is not a case you build against yourself. It isn't an ugly mental picture or a hardened view of what you are really like. It is the clear, unwavering recognition that you have thoughts and impulses that are abhorrent to you. Disliking your ego in this way immediately spurs you to begin letting it go.

Letting Go of Prediction and Control

ave you heard this one?

So far today I haven't cursed another driver. I haven't eaten too much sugar or fat. No family member has disagreed with me even once. And nothing embarrassing has happened at work.

Things are working out pretty well so far.

But now it's time to get out of bed.

At least we have control of when we get out of bed.

Don't we?

Be careful how you answer this, because if you fail to answer it honestly, to some degree you will be a victim of every suggestion you overhear today, whether it comes from the mouth of your TV or the mouth of your worst enemy. You also will become potential prey for success books, advice articles, and talk show experts. You might even pay good money to hear a motivational speaker tell you there's a way to "get control of your life."

Therefore, kindly permit me to repeat the question: Do you control when you get out of bed?

Or, do you think, "I should get up now," then notice that you lie there a moment or two longer.

Ah, but do you then get up when you decide?

Or, do you hit the snooze button and think, "Well, maybe I'll rest here a moment or two"—then notice that you immediately get up. Or perhaps rest many more than "a moment or two." In fact, I'll bet there was a time when you stayed in bed most of the day, thinking all the while that you should get up.

What never happens is that you think, "Now I'm going to get up," and rise the exact instant that thought comes to mind.

In other words, do we control even this simplest of all outcomes? We are the only factor we have to deal with in this first decision of the day. I'm assuming, of course, that your sheets aren't tucked too tight or your partner doesn't suddenly get a lustful thought and grab you. Add just one other factor—a virus, a leg cramp, your kid jumping on you—and you know you aren't in control.

Let's say we're not yet talking about the interference of other factors. Even given other factors, you probably will succeed in getting out of bed. But do you determine the exact moment you arise, the position of your limbs, the feeling in your joints and muscles, which foot steps on the hairball the cat threw up, or your overall mood when you finally make it out? Do you even control which thoughts you will be thinking once you are standing on your own two feet?

Before we consider the question of whether we can control our lives, let's be honest about this much simpler question: Does anyone control this most basic of all acts—starting the day? Because if we truly can't control that, we can't control anything. I'm here to say we can't control anything. This is why being single doesn't give us independence, why having personal wealth doesn't give us protection, why having raised our children doesn't set us free, or any of the zillion other conclusions our culture draws from the assumption that the key to control is to rely on ourselves first. Yet when we do consider ourself first, what are we considering?

Letting Go of I, Me, and Mine

If we close our eyes and try to go to that place within our heart where we feel stillness and peace, we can always find it; it is always there. That part of us has no control issues. It is another part of us—the ego mind or conflicted mind—that looks for what must be controlled next.

Most of us think of this other part as "I," "me," or "mine." When we ask "ourselves" what we want, we are really consulting only this part. Yet we work unrelentingly on its behalf, Not only do we protect its "boundaries," we closely monitor the respect and acknowledgement it receives. We vigilantly watch the gauge of each of its cravings to see whether "we" need filling.

Yet, ironically, no one controls the formation of the "me" that wants us to control! We work for a tyrant we didn't elect.

Although the set of needs the "me" contains differs with each individual, we blindly give our own set priority over our life partners, children, friends, professions, and overall happiness. Devoting ourselves exclusively to meeting our needs is such a narrow, paltry, petty approach to living that it is virtual death. Yet we do this without ever asking why we would want to control on behalf of something we never controlled in the first place.

Of the thousands of factors that combined to shape "us," our ego, our worldly identity, we didn't determined a single one. We didn't control the emotional state our parents were in when they conceived us. The time of month. Which sperm won the race. How the genes combined. What our mother ate, drank, and did during gestation. When her water broke. The time it took to get to the hospital. What bumps the car went over. Who was on duty. How long the delivery lasted. Which method was used to get us out. Where the heavenly bodies were positioned. How long we were left unattended in the nursery. Whether we were first- or second-born. If, when, and for how long we were breastfed.

And I haven't even gotten to "the formative years"!

We didn't control any of it. Not one factor that went into the formation of the particular "me" we think we are was of our choosing. Yet we are driven by the psychology and philosophy of our culture to devote all our hearts, souls, and minds to getting everything this "me" we didn't make wants.

Hugh and Gayle

Just before my third date with Gayle, my two roommates asked me if I was getting serious about her. I was appalled by their question. As I explained, Gayle and I hardly knew each other—we had spent a total of eight hours together! I pointed out that Gayle had the wrong politics. She had the wrong religion. She smoked, drank, and ate junk food. She had been seen on a motorcycle. In summary I said, "Would you get serious about someone who listened to country music?"

A few hours later, Gayle and I were parked across the street from a coffeehouse trying to decide whether we wanted to go in. The conversation went like this:

"Would you like to do something else?" (me)

"Well, I guess so." (Gayle).

"Would you like to get married?" (me)

"Well, I guess so." (Gayle)

We lived in Dallas and you had to wait three days to get married. An hour later we were driving toward the Oklahoma border where you could get married on the spot.

About halfway there, Gayle asked, "Do you think this is going to work out?"

"No," I said. "Do you think it's going to work out?"

"No," she said.

So we kept driving toward Oklahoma, where, a couple of hours later we got married.

On the way back to her place, Gayle said, "I hope you realize no piece of paper gives any man the right to my body"—whereupon she disappeared into her apartment and wouldn't see me for two weeks.

How we became writers is a similar story.

How we had our first child is a similar story.

How we became ministers is a similar story. But you get the point.

Thirty-five years later we have three wonderful sons (one by a previous marriage). We have five wonderful pets. This is our fifteenth book. We serve a church that did not ordain us. We live in a city that can get above 115 degrees in the summer. And in the last four nights, we have killed ninety-three adult scorpions living in a tight circle around our house. (We don't talk about what happened to their babies.)

Like most people's lives—some good, some bad. Like everyone's life—no control.

> *Some things are simple, and here's one of them:*
> *You can either relax and let go of your life, in*
> *which case you will know peace. Or you can try to*
> *control your life, in which case you will know war.*

release 11

Suggested time: 2 or more days

A. At the start of the day, when you first become aware that you are waking up, notice when you decide to get out of bed and notice when you actually get out of bed.

B. At some point later that same day, ask yourself what will you be doing in five minutes. Be quite specific:

"What category of activity will I be engaged in?"

"What will be my body's general position or movement?"

"What kind of thoughts will I be thinking?"

"What overall mood will I be in?

Then set a watch or timer to go off in five minutes. When the time is up, compare what you thought you would be doing to what you are doing.

C. I recommend that you do the entire exercise each day for at least two consecutive days.

Remember, in this Release we're only talking about whether we can predict five minutes ahead. Yet we think nothing of asking ourselves—or our friends!—whether we should marry MoRay, who we met by accident while waiting to get a molar filled; or, instead, move to Terre Haute, which was profiled in *All About Me* magazine in the same waiting room.

release 12

Suggested time: 2 days or more

- Throughout the next two days—and, ideally, in the days and weeks to come—notice how frequently small, routine tasks and events do not proceed as you would reasonably expect. For example, if you happen to leave both bread and crackers out on your kitchen counter, the next morning the bread will be hard and the crackers will be soft! This Release requires a different focus of your attention than perhaps you are in the habit of giving. We are so used to chaos that we overlook it most of the time. Yet only by overlooking it can we sustain a belief that there is a way to control events and other egos.

During these two days, closely watch your body perform familiar tasks—ones you have been doing all your life. As you tie a shoe, turn on a lamp, pick a scrap of paper off the floor, comb your hair, pour a bowl of cereal, and the like, ask yourself if everything that is happening during the course of this one small event is logical and expected.

release 13

Suggested time: 1 or more days

Please allow me to remind you of what I said earlier: You will reap more benefit from each Release if you will not attempt more than one a day. Each Release requires a different focus and mixing focuses diminishes the insight each one offers. With that in mind:

- Before you go to sleep, make a note of the following words and put it where you will see it when you wake to start your day:

  "Nothing will go right today. So I will relax and be amused." This somewhat odd goal for the day merely puts into practice what we have been discussing; namely, that the key to mental freedom is to see the world exactly as it is and then to gently decline any call from within ourselves or outside ourselves to get caught up in trying to change its basic nature. Naturally, this doesn't mean we never make changes that would benefit our loved ones or ourselves. Everything we do—even yawning or soaking in a tub of warm water—changes something. Potentially, though, any change can be made peacefully. This is not a political statement, a call for pacifism, or the impossible ideal that head lice and other living creatures should never be killed. It's a simple observation that we can walk gently toward Home, or we can claw our way there, kicking and screaming about each small distance we have to traverse.

Letting Go of Outcomes

Although we can't control even the tiniest ego or smallest event, we can control our decision to control. We can let go and be free, or we can fight useless battles. But we can't do both. Either our attention is on form or content, on appearance or substance. By letting go of our desire to dominate outcomes, we don't sacrifice anything real, but we do open our heart and mind to the experience of wholeness.

An example of control that looks like love but causes separation is the policy in many homes of a forced "family time" or a required "family dinner." If these times are welcomed by all involved, then naturally they are not examples of control. Mandated events can indeed create a picture of oneness— everyone now is together in the living room playing Boggle or sitting at the table eating corn on the cob. Forcing this picture is often done at the expense of true love and unity.

Likewise, when one partner pressures the other partner to call from work more often, have sex more often, or to talk about "How did your day go?" instead of watching TV, the result may be an increased appearance of affection, but at the price of increased distance and separation. Control, because it contains elements of war, simply cannot lead to an expansion of love.

Becka and Larry

A couple of years ago Gayle and I counseled a couple named Becka and Larry who had a problem that about 90 percent of all the couples we see have—their sex drives were not identical. Larry wanted sex two to three times a week. Becka wanted sex one or two times a month. Their compromise was to have sex every Saturday night whether either of them were in the mood or not. Further complicating the situation was Larry's belief that Becka's not wanting to have sex as often as he did meant she didn't love him, and Becka's belief that Larry's need to masturbate was a form of infidelity.

First, we asked them to take turns saying something they loved about the other person until they had each said ten things. This simple exercise will usually shift each partner's focus from what they are not getting to what they are getting, from their conflicted minds to their peaceful minds, from their separateness to their connectedness. The moment the shift takes place is always obvious: the couple becomes happy. They smile; they laugh; they may even giggle.

The next thing we asked Larry and Becka to do was to close their eyes, look in their hearts, and ask themselves what purpose they wanted sex to serve in their marriage; what they wanted their motive for having it to be; and what effect they wanted the sex act to have on their relationship.

Although Larry kept his eyes closed longer than Becka, they essentially told us the same thing—they wanted sex to be an act of love and they wanted it to be something that brought them closer together.

As you've probably noticed, writers always cite their successes, and, admittedly, our session with this couple went about as smoothly as these things can go, because the next thing Becka said was, "Well, I guess we need to change this from a running argument to a running love-fest." And Larry, in a moment of groundless euphoria we knew he would regret later, said, "Honey, I don't ever want you to have sex again when you don't want it." We all ignored that comment.

Having all this good will to work with, Gayle and I were able to be realistic and practical. One of the things Gayle said to Larry was, "Have you ever had a wonderful meal and stuffed yourself so full you just couldn't eat another bite?"

"All too often," Larry answered.

"Think how you would feel if every time you finished a meal like that Becka said to you, 'Larry, I want you to eat another meal the same size, and if you really love me you will do it right now.' As a woman, I can tell you that's what it feels like to think of having sex when you don't want it."

For my part, I tried to explain to Becka one difference in how most men's urge to have sex differs from most women's. As semen builds up in their bodies, men feel a growing need to release it. If they can somehow tough this out long enough, the semen will eventually come out in a wet dream. But, I told her, although I knew they existed, I had never met a man who could hold out that long. So you see, I said to Becka, asking Larry only to have sex twice a month—and yet not to masturbate—is like his asking you only to eat once every two or three days, yet never have a snack.

The outcome of the session was that Larry and Becka decided to help each other with their separate sexual rhythms. Later that week Becka gave Larry of box of "masturbatory facilitators" that her friend who worked at a fertility clinic suggested, plus one weekly "free pass" that Larry could cash in for sex on demand.

Larry granted Becka "five wishes" for how he could make their sexual times better for her. They also both agreed to begin doing research on other ways they could have erotic exchanges that didn't involve formal intercourse. Even more importantly, they agreed that if what they tried at first didn't solve the problem, they would keep trying other approaches until they hit upon one that worked. In other words, they agreed to out-endure the problem.

Later, they told us that after a few false starts they worked out a "fairly pleasant" approach, and that sex was no longer the dividing issue it used to be. I wish I could report fabulous sex ever after, but a pleasant sex life, with only a few hitches along the way, is a definite success.

Obviously, not every couple will solve this problem as quickly as Becka and Larry, but it is instructive to understand what allowed them to solve it:

1. They stopped trying to control each other.

2. They switched their focus from thoughts that separated them to thoughts that connected them. Note that these were thoughts they already had, not just words about thoughts they would like to have.

3. Looking at each other affectionately, they saw that they wanted to make life easier on each other, and so they studied each other's needs—something even a loving pet owner would not hesitate to do.

4. They made a tentative plan and tried it—with the understanding that if parts of it didn't work, they would keep trying until they found a combination that did work.

To summarize: You can't control other egos and events, so let go of control. You can only control your focus. So focus on what unites, comforts, and stills your mind. If there is a thought blocking this focus, look closely at it until you see that it is not what you believe most deeply—but this must be seen, not just said. You will know when you have seen what you believe most deeply because it will make you happy. It will always show you your connection and unity with the people around you.

Letting Go of Inner Conflict

I am aware that to ask you to identify disturbing thoughts as an essential step toward cleansing your mind runs counter to current values. At the moment, our culture places great stock in the art of being disturbing.

This high regard extends even to books, plays, news specials, and the like. In reviews, a "deeply disturbing" movie or book is one that supposedly has meaning, depth, and relevance. Jolting musical groups, shocking talk shows, and volatile athletes are rewarded financially. Those public figures who coat themselves in adversarial rhetoric and polarizing opinions receive the media's brightest spotlight. Ministers, teachers, and TV commentators often profess that they want their message to disturb. They say, "I want to shake the audience out of its apathy." Their assumption is that the more they disturb their listeners, the more likely their listeners are to "use their minds."

It is stillness, not disturbance, that plumbs the depths of our mind. If we want to know our deepest beliefs, hear our intuition, and remember our love for the people in our lives, agitated thoughts are of little use to us. Perhaps it was the recognition that Truth is seen only in stillness and that peace is experienced only in peace, which gave rise to the ancient Chinese curse, "May you live in interesting times."

As I mentioned earlier, when we are disturbed we have the illusion of doing something meaningful. We think that our upset is an accomplishment in itself. For example, every newspaper has its editorial and op-ed sections. Those who read these regularly are often considered "deeper" thinkers than those who don't. Yet few papers contain a section of equal length giving steps the reader can take toward solving the problems highlighted. To the ego part of our mind, getting upset, deciding who to blame, or taking "a strong stand" is sufficient. Note that few people leave a disturbing movie determined to do something about the issue presented. They walk out animated to talk about it.

At present we are a people addicted to a good fight. We don't particularly care where we have to go to find one. Watching or reading fictional conflicts is satisfying. Seeing reports of real ones is even better. But embroiling ourselves in one disturbance after another is best.

This being the atmosphere we live in, I realize it may take a leap of faith to do the Releases in this book. Remember, all you are being asked is to experience mental wholeness, not a controlled countenance and rigid conduct; mental stillness, not softly spoken words and a flat affect; mental peace, not timid stands and shaky loyalties. Everything in this book is meant to address inner healing and release, not the picture you present to the world.

If you walk gently through your resistance and do the Releases as conscientiously as possible, you will see that holding onto mental disturbance of any kind is of no benefit to you or anyone you love. Inner turmoil is a great cacophony that keeps you from hearing your real thoughts and experiencing your real feelings. Sweep it from your mind and the peace that takes its place is like the sounds of the morning, only this time, you are the gently rising sun, the opening leaves, the singing birds.

Letting Go of Relationship Battles You Aren't Having

Perhaps nowhere else can our belief that being disturbed is a sufficient goal be seen more clearly than in our romantic relationships. The time and energy we spend vainly attempting to convince our partner that we are right is staggering. Even though arguing is a cooperative venture, few couples make a comparable effort, or any effort at all, to move their relationship past an issue. What they care about most is how tellingly they present their side of the schism.

For most of the hundreds of couples Gayle and I counsel each year, the disturbances between them are far more meaningful than their friendship. They speak of how upset they are, or how their upset is not being "honored," or how their partner gets too upset or not upset enough, or how they are not allowed to be upset in the way they wish. Much of their time away from each other is spent obsessing on their upsets. They read books and magazines and watch talk shows that dissect various kinds of upsets. The friends and relatives with whom they discuss all this invariably add upset on top of upset.

The generally preferred solution to relationship turmoil is to "bail." The term *bail* or *bail out* originally meant to parachute from a disabled aircraft. The plane goes down but you land safely on your feet. Sounds great, but here again, human beings' tendency to settle for mere appearances comes into play.

When people divorce, they may separate bodies, children, and finances, but rarely do they separate their minds from this failed relationship. Actually, most people do the opposite. They build a detailed case against their former partner and tell it to everyone, as if nourishing judgments, grievances, and grudges were a path to mental health and freedom. All they do is sharpen and plunge the damaging thoughts as deeply into their psyches as they can. As a result, they carry very powerful thoughts about what was done to them into their next relationship.

As a counselor, you sit there and listen to a woman yell at Stewart, her last partner, although Fred, her new partner, is the one she is looking at. And she doesn't even know she's doing this. You watch a young man relate to his mother when he thinks he's relating to his girlfriend. Indeed, his relationship with his mother was a failed relationship, but he can't see that the one he is in now doesn't have to fail. These are emotion addictions in the truest sense. An old pattern is in place and the "addict" is a victim of his or her past, not the present.

Substance abusers quickly reach the stage at which the substance doesn't have the effect it used to. Consequently, they don't like it any more. They may even hate it. But they are helpless before the chemical patterns that have been set up in their bodies. With couples, the inner patterns are mental, but they are every bit as overpowering and self-sustaining.

Those who take any one of a hundred mind-altering drugs can see reality change before their eyes. A pleasant picture on the wall and a normal person sitting on the other side of the room can both begin to look sinister to the drug user. The drug doesn't cause a mere suspicion that these things may be sinister; it alters their features and the drug user has objective proof that they are sinister. Cause and effect become obvious when the drug wears off and the drug user sees what actually occurred—that is, until the addiction forces another episode.

However, when a new relationship is seen through the lens of an old relationship, the cause of the distortion is not obvious; nor does it end in a few minutes or hours. Each new relationship failure reinforces the distortion, and eventually the place where hearts are joined can no longer be experienced.

It is quite sad to see how many relationship crises today are not about the relationship; they are about thoughts of old relationships. These couples don't have a chance. They can't even experience the potential of the new relationship because they aren't in it.

Please understand that this cannot be helped as long as powerful thoughts about what went on with Stewart or with Mom are active. Somehow people believe it's enough to recognize that they shouldn't "carry baggage" into their new relationship. Yet their hands have convulsed and locked around the handles, and unless they become deeply aware, the baggage is now permanently a part of them.

The other side of this coin is that those who do become aware gain their freedom. No matter how powerfully you were influenced or damaged by any previous relationship, whether with parents, peers, or an ex-spouse, if you work diligently to bring the thoughts your mind still carries into full awareness, you eventually become free to choose how you will feel and act.

An example of how this process occurs naturally can be seen in how differently people act out the racial, sexual, financial, and other group prejudices they pick up in childhood. In each area of the country there are strong feelings against certain groups. The particular groups singled out differ from location to location, and many people who travel have been amused to hear almost identical criticisms directed at Native Americans in Santa Fe, Mexicans in Dallas, Koreans in L.A., and Puerto Ricans in New York. These groups are so unlike each other that obviously "the locals" are seeing their prejudices, not the groups.

Most likely, some form of prejudice was part of the atmosphere you took in daily, if not in your home, then in your neighborhood or the schools you attended. If you are like most people, your basic mindset contains echoes of those prejudices even today, regardless whether you see intellectually that they are unreasonable.

If you are hiring for your company and an applicant who is a member of the group that was disliked when you were a child walks through the door, your immediate impression of this person might very well be distorted by prejudice. By being aware of this attitude and knowing where it came from, you can quickly concentrate on not letting it continue to distort your view of someone who might very well be an asset to the company. If anything, your awareness motivates you to take pains to be especially fair with this person.

Another example concerns the generalized opinions men have about women, and that women have about men, which they laugh about and bemoan among themselves. When it comes to the individual they are dating, most people are conscious enough to set aside these attitudes and see the person clearly.

In both examples, I'm sure you know people who are sufficiently unconscious of their prejudices and let these thoughts affect their ability to see a job applicant or the person they are considering dating to the point that they pass up a good prospect. They actually think that the person before them is as flawed as the way they view the group from which this individual comes.

You can see that they are unaware of what is motivating them. Perhaps you have discovered that pointing out their mistake doesn't work. It doesn't work because they have to want to become aware, and they have to make the effort themselves.

Many people see the tragic effects of unconscious motivation all around them; still they won't take the time to cleanse their minds of destructive pollutants. They may be aware of how often failed relationships have negative effects on the lives of their friends and acquaintances, yet they believe that somehow they are not similarly affected.

We may sense that we have not released an old relationship completely, but since this residue is in our mind—which can't be seen—all that matters is that we talk as if we have. We make it plain to friends, relatives, and complete strangers that we'll "never again have anything to do with" this former spouse or that former lover. We "can't stomach them." They "make us sick." We "shudder at the thought" of them. We're "lucky to be alive." They "need help." They're "really very sick." We "feel sorry" for them. We "pity" them. We've "learned our lesson." We're "glad to be out of it." We're "never going to make that mistake again."

Yet how can you believe that you were thrown into a fire and then believe you didn't get burned? When you are burned, that part of the body becomes very sensitive to heat. In fact, it overreacts to heat. You can't tolerate a degree of warmth that really is not harming you because it feels like it's harming you. Your new partner isn't doing what the old partner did, but it feels like she or he is.

After a failed relationship, your mind now has a number of burned places, places where you were yelled at, undercut, told you were crazy, betrayed, belittled, lied to, manipulated, or bullied. Anything that even looks like that, is that. Furthermore, if you believe it's how you're being treated again, you will act on that belief. You will destroy or cripple the new relationship.

If you take nothing else from this book, please take this: If you believe it, you will act on it. If

> *you continue believing it, you will act on it again*
> *and again.*

Of course it's possible that it is happening all over again. Despite all the books that tell you that you keep "attracting" these kind of people, based on the twenty-five years Gayle and I have been counseling couples, that almost never is the case. There are definitely new conflicts, but these are not the old conflicts. Unfortunately, the new conflicts never get addressed.

So what do you do about the thoughts you have about your failed relationships? You expose the thoughts and let them go. This is true whatever the relationship was that failed— whether with a parent, sibling, lover, friend, or with the father or mother of your children.

release 14

Suggested time: 1 or more days

- This Release requires deep honesty and detailed attention. Therefore, set aside twenty minutes or more and go to a place where you won't be interrupted. Take something to write with and make yourself comfortable. Your inner depth of vision will increase if you can have a sustained period of quiet.

- At this time, consider only one failed relationship, the earliest one in your life. Consider the relationship a failure if any important aspect of it failed. Naturally, for most people this will be a parent or guardian. If you consider the relationships with both your parents a failure in some important way, begin with the parent who you believe affected you the most. That person could very well be the parent who wasn't around—who abandoned the family, who merely donated sperm, who got lost in a career, or who was emotionally distant. For instance, if one of your parents ran off with someone else, you can't help having deep thoughts about it which affect your current relationship.

I realize that it's not popular to think of relationships with a parent, an adult child, or a long-term spouse as failures. The current ideal is to say that all experiences are lessons if we could just see them that way. Note how inconsistent we are in applying this ideal. We have no trouble seeing a failed business, a failed kidney, a failed dishwasher, or even a flat tire as things that failed. Obviously there are failed relationships. No parent or spouse starts out wanting a relationship to deteriorate into crisis and chaos. Something can be an admitted failure and still many helpful lessons may come out of it. In truth, we learn more quickly and deeply if we look honestly at our own and other people's mistakes.

- Start with your earliest memory of this relationship and go through everything that happened in chronological order. If the relationship is still active, continue up to the present. If at some point the relationship turned around and became uniformly positive, continue to the end of the negative period only.

Look carefully at any event that still disturbs you in any way. Recall the emotions you felt and, if you can, the thoughts you had during the disturbance, and write these down. Then go to the next event.

• It would be good not to have more than two of these twenty-minute-plus sessions a day. However, do this for as many days as necessary to cover the period of this one relationship.

• When you have worked your way through to the end, read your lists of thoughts in one sitting and write a summary of the central attitude or thought that you see running through this list. This will be your T-thought, or one of them. (See Release 6, page 68, and Release 10, page 97, for lists of typical T-thoughts.)

release 15

Suggested time: 1 or more days

• After completing Release 14, skip to your most recent failed romantic relationship as an adult. Follow the same procedure used in Release 14.

• After reading through and summarizing your list of thoughts for this most recent romantic relationship, compare this summary to the summary you wrote for Release 14. Try to write a single thought that covers both summaries. For example, if your summarizing thought from Release 14 was "I'm always the one who causes the trouble," and your summarizing thought from Release 15 was "No matter what I do, it's never enough," a thought that might cover both could be "I am always causing everyone trouble because I never hold up my end of things." This, of course, would be your T-thought stated in more detail.

Release 14 and 15 are largely exercises in intuition. You are trying to sense what attitude you picked up in an early relationship (say, with your father), then sense how this came out in a later relationship (say, with your last lover). There is no perfect way to do this and no perfect outcome. However, it would be impossible to do this work without making meaningful gains in awareness. Awareness, more than any other factor, is the key to cleansing your mind and making it whole.

Maggie

A woman named Maggie e-mailed Gayle and said that about six months ago she began noticing that she was sad after her weekly phone conversation with her mother. Gayle asked her if this had ever happened before. Maggie said no, and that furthermore her mother was very healthy and nothing unusual had happened recently in her mother's life.

Gayle told Maggie that for the next two weeks she wanted her to sit down with paper and pen immediately after each call, and, while concentrating on her feeling of sadness, to write down every thought in her mind.

Two weeks later, Maggie e-mailed back that the words *loser* and *You're a loser* kept recurring in her mind. "But," she said, "my mother is not a loser. She's a very popular schoolteacher who has won an award. And I have a great career as a physical therapist and don't consider myself a loser either."

Gayle told Maggie to sit quietly once or twice in the next few days and trace back all her memories surrounding the word *loser.* She also told her to write down her thoughts after one more phone conversation with her mother.

The next week Maggie e-mailed Gayle again, this time very excited about what she had discovered. Six months before, her father, who had divorced her mother when Maggie was ten, had come into town and they had had lunch together. At that time her father told her that he had divorced her mother because "she was such a loser," having no career goal higher than to be a schoolteacher. Maggie's father was a doctor and had run off with another doctor.

Gayle asked Maggie if there was any aspect of her own life that had not been successful. Maggie replied that she was thirty-seven and had never been able to form a permanent relationship. She said that the man she was dating now wanted to get married but that something was holding her back. He was a wonderful man but she felt very reluctant.

Again Gayle advised Maggie to sit in the middle of the emotion and write down all her thoughts, this time whenever she felt this familiar reluctance.

In their next-to-last exchange, Maggie told Gayle that the thought she uncovered was quite crazy. "It was, 'If I get married, I will become a loser.' How could I have such a thought?" Gayle replied, "Because you lived for many years in a house where your father held the deep conviction that your own mother was a loser. You are half your dad and half your mother, so naturally you are going to internalize this loser thought—which proved powerful enough to break apart your home."

In her last e-mail, Maggie told Gayle that she and her boyfriend had discussed the work she had been doing and he was very supportive. Although they had not yet decided to get married, she had invited him to move in. They were going to see how it went.

Like Maggie's story, most of the people Gayle and I work with identify a generalized, long-term experience in childhood rather than a single traumatic event as the root of their T-thought. For instance, a woman named Anna saw clearly that she was never wanted by her parents and thus had the T-thought that she was not really wanted at any party, any workplace, and not even by the members of her immediate family.

A man named Douglas with whom we worked traced his T-thought of "I will never succeed" back to his father and grandfather, both of whom "taught" their sons, "You will never be the man I am."

A woman named Lorrin was eight when her mother died. She then spent ten years being cared for haphazardly and inadequately by her older brother. As a result, Lorrin developed the T-thought, "You can't rely on anyone."

The fact that all these T-thoughts are irrational is not a coincidence. T-thoughts are usually second- or third-generation thoughts and the circumstances from which they arose do not coincide with present circumstances. For instance, a good friend of mine, Mike Michelson, said, "My T-thought has been passed down like a virus within my father's side of the family. It is 'Michelsons are superior to everyone including other Michelsons.' There is nothing I know of in our family's history that supports Michelson superiority. But I assume that somewhere in the past something happened to spawn this thought. In recent times, it has been completely out of context—but that hasn't weakened it in the least."

As in Mike's case, all T-thoughts are invulnerable to reason. Only the deeper understandings of the heart can spotlight and weaken them. Gayle and I have never known anyone who had a completely reasonable T-thought. This characteristic of

T-thoughts often slows people's ability to recognize them. They just can't believe that something as ridiculous as "My dad thought my mother was a loser; therefore I will become a loser if I get married" could account for fifteen years of inability to commit.

We have to look at our childhood and its effect on our mind as it is. Our childhood is over. Our mind is now our responsibility. It only delays our mental freedom to say, "It shouldn't have happened." Of course it shouldn't have. But it did.

> *Don't waste your time judging your parents. They had parents too.*

Observe how often people discuss what their parents did to them in a tone of outrage. This is merely a form of procrastination. We all make this mistake, but eventually we must recognize that the only meaningful questions to ask about our past are, "When am I going to accept that what happened, happened?" And, "When am I going to accept responsibility for the ego I have?" Once you take this stand, you now are ready to practice and extend your wholeness.

release 16

This Release is specifically for those who have had a long string of failed romantic relationships. Unless your partner died, the relationship failed if you are no longer in it. Of course, this doesn't imply that there were not good reasons for getting out. However, if time and again you thought that you and another person were committed, yet that commitment ended, it's quite likely that something more than bad luck is operating.

One sign that you are participating in these breakups is a similarity in how most of them ended. For instance: You are usually the one who leaves. The other person usually leaves. The other person is usually married or in another relationship. The ending is usually about sex. The ending is usually about emotional abuse. The ending is usually about money. The ending is usually about a lack of commitment from the other person.

Endings may also be similar even though they are not overtly the same. Your emotional buildup or reaction may be the common factor: Some mannerism—a way of walking, talking, eating, dressing—becomes so annoying that either you must leave or make of it a relationship-ending issue. Something about the way the other person looks—some facial feature, for example—grows into a huge turn-off for you. Something about the other person's conversations—the subject matter they center on, the way they analyze or fail to analyze, their cultural or political literacy—becomes something you negatively obsess over. Or a familiar emotion starts building up in you—a need to move on and be free; a growing uneasiness, nervousness or generalized distress; a growing fear set off by your seeing more and more "red flags"; a growing hopelessness; a growing distrust.

Although there will always be one or two endings that were exceptions, the indicator is the similarity of the endings. Each potential partner was a separate person, and if most of the endings were alike in action or feeling, this signals the operation of a T-thought.

Many people are so unconscious of their T-thoughts that they don't see a similarity in the way their relationships end until they begin taking a closer look. The following exercise has proven to be highly effective in uncovering the particular thought that takes over feelings and perceptions and assures that each new relationship will fail. The key to the success of this Release is your willingness to do it in its entirety.

- Beginning with your most recent failed romantic relationship (unless you covered this in Release 15), start with the first disturbing feeling or event that occurred and review it in as much detail as you can. Write out everything you can remember about this first little hitch or big upset. As you recount the circumstances surrounding a feeling you had or the details of an event, write down every thought that you can remember being in your mind at that time.

- Having thoroughly reviewed this first disturbance, go back and take each thought you recorded, and, in turn, trace each one as far back as you can. What happened just before the disturbance that this thought reminds you of? What happened before that? And so on, as far back into your life as you can remember.

It's important not to analyze what any thought means. You are interested only in what you can see. Once you see nothing more, take up the next thought that you recorded, and continue in this same way until all the recorded thoughts for this first upset have been traced backward.

- Take the next disturbing feeling or event that occurred in this first failed relationship and work through it in the same way. Keep doing this until everything in that relationship has been covered.

- Then take up your second most recent romantic relationship and proceed in the same way. Continue with each relationship back to and including the first one that failed.

- Read through everything you have written, in one sitting if possible. The unconscious thoughts that have controlled you will be as plain as day.

Terry

A man named Terry had a history of broken relationships. When we talked, he was once again dating someone he was about to dump. After writing down every thought he recalled having within each stage of their history together, he saw that his dominant emotion had slowly evolved into aversion toward her, coupled with a need to get away that bordered on panic.

In the course of searching his mind for thoughts he had had in each of his other failed relationships, Terry suddenly remembered himself as an adolescent, watching his mother doing the laundry, and thinking, "She will never have the right partner." This memory struck him as odd since his mother had then been, and still was, married to his father.

Tracing this memory as far back as he could, Terry remembered something his mother had confided in him several years before the laundry scene. She said that she had been engaged to the most wonderful man, who had died in an accident. Shortly after that tragedy, she met his father and a year later they were married. She added, "Your dad was handsome in those days." Obviously she had married second best.

Suddenly he recognized the deeply held T-thought that

had sabotaged all his relationships. It was, "This is not the right person because I can only have second best." This thought was not even his belief; it was his mother's belief. As usually happens to all of us during childhood, he had absorbed many of the deep thoughts of his parents as if they were his own.

Terry was now alert to his true motivation in ending relationships. It was to avoid second best. Now began the long process of weeding this thought out of every unhelpful impulse that was occurring in his current relationship and in his life. He carefully examined his thoughts each time he withdrew from, criticized, or doubted his partner or anyone else. Eventually, he was able to stop himself from acting these thoughts out.

Time and again Terry saw that behind each impulse to separate was his desire to avoid second best. Recognizing this gave him a choice in his current relationship that he had not had before. When a negative feeling about his partner was active, he could say, "Yes, that's my programmed feeling, but what is my true feeling?" He would then become still and look in his heart to see what he really felt. Recognizing this deeper attitude, he was free to extend it, instead of his mother's attitude.

At this time Terry has made enormous strides, but he is not yet out of the woods. The problem is that his feelings of aversion toward his partner feel honest and true and his efforts to look at them seem dangerous. Seeing where an emotion comes from does not eliminate the emotion. We have to take the further step of accessing a deeper, truer thought and practice responding from it. Fortunately, Terry has a partner who is patient and willing to work with him, and his prospect for complete freedom from his old mindset is excellent.

Letting Go of Useless Blocks to Relationship

In doing Special Needs Release 16, you create a state of mind that is ready for a permanent, happy relationship. You see what blocks your commitment, and this provides you with the option to commit. All that is left is to practice committing.

Naturally, if you don't already have one, you will need a partner—and this means you are limited to those available. Since that is the reality, why not broaden your pool of potential partners? Is it truly not spiritual or "somehow not right" to avail yourself of personal ads, Internet postings, dating services, and regular visits to places and events where the kind of person you are looking for is most likely to be?

We wouldn't dream of relying on random luck when buying a present for a loved one, looking for a place to live, or finding new clothes for a wedding or a trip. Of course we all hear stories of a great job or such just dropping into someone's lap. In a world of chaos, these things happen. But it's silly to say that it's somehow more spiritual, more natural, or shows more faith in God to wait for all things important to come to us. And no one does this in any consistent way.

We look through the bananas, squeeze the avocados, and tap the watermelons. At least we walk in the store and find the right aisle. People will even do research and "shop around" when looking for a child to adopt. When it comes to finding a good partner, somehow the universe, the mystical law of soul-mates, or God is supposed to provide delivery service. If there are useless battles that can be let go of, this kind of self-imposed impediment to companionship is certainly one of them.

Letting Go of Sticky Thoughts

If you have spent even a little time observing your thoughts, you have noticed that a parade of images and ideas passes non-stop through your mind. Most of these random thoughts pass before the mind's eye and out of range of your interest quite quickly. However, a few do not.

From time to time a thought catches our attention and we begin "chewing" on it. This preoccupation splits the mind and we experience a loss of wholeness.

I'm going to make several assumptions about sticky thoughts—thoughts that grab our interest—that have proven helpful in the process of letting go. These assumptions may or may not be obvious to you after doing the first fifteen or sixteen Releases, but they should become increasingly so as we proceed.

- Any thought we do not believe or don't think is important will not disrupt our wholeness and peace.

- Any thought that preoccupies us will produce disrupting emotions (fear, anger, worry, hatred, discouragement, anxiety, jealousy, and the like).

- Thoughts that produce these emotions cause us to make poor and conflicted decisions that skew our lives in harmful directions.

- All thoughts that produce disrupting emotions have large unconscious aspects—that is, we are seeing only part of the thought.

- The unconscious aspect of the thought causes our fascination with or addiction to the thought.

- Whenever we experience a disrupting emotion, part of what we think is unconscious, so merely adding positive or "spiritual" thoughts does not work, and further shatters the mind.

- The unconscious part—not the conscious part—of the thought dictates which emotions we feel.

- To fixate on a thought—no matter what it is—is a choice we make in the present. We are free to reverse this choice whenever we wish.

- One way to release a preoccupying thought is to make it fully conscious. Once we see the thought in its entirety, we will not believe it, will not want it, and will gladly let it go.

release 17

Suggested time: 1 or more days

As long as we stand on the side and quietly watch a parade go by, we cause no problems for ourselves. However, if we leave the ranks of spectators and begin running after some cartoon figure, we ask for trouble. Likewise, when we chase some random thought that crosses our mind, we immediately initiate a useless mental ruckus.

- Today and tomorrow, practice what we hope will be the beginning of a lifelong habit. Whenever you have a quiet moment, peacefully and attentively watch each thought that enters your mind and any emotion that trails behind it. Watch as it passes by, then go to the next thought, and the next. Your only goal is to look in comfort, to see clearly each product on the production line of the ego mind, and to respond only with peace. Don't attack, judge, worship, or pursue any thought or emotion. Just acknowledge its presence and watch what comes next.

- In the course of being the peaceful spectator, you may notice a place within your awareness where you are already still and happy. It is like a lake of illumination or a land of serenity, and it is bathed in welcome. Whenever you wish, you can safely immerse yourself in the lake, walk gently upon the land, and take the welcome into your heart. This is the one place that makes the parade of thoughts wholly irrelevant. In this place you can safely ignore them all. Go to this place often and pause in stillness within the gentle light of the Divine.

Letting Go of Gloom

In doing Release 17, perhaps you sensed that another excellent way to let go of conflicts is to immerse your mind in stillness. It really doesn't matter whether we pick each pollutant from our mind one by one through awareness or flood our mind with purity because the outcome is the same: an unconflicted mind. However, having the option of both conscious cleansing and immersion is useful, because there will be times when some disrupting thought will have such a grip on our mind that it must be released before immersion will even be possible. There will also be other times when our mind is in a receptive state, so that digging for still one more mental pollutant isn't necessary.

Our problem is not that we lack the ability to cleanse our minds. In fact, we flush them of many memories and lines of thought throughout the day and night. But we usually do this unconsciously.

Deliberately using our capacity to be amused is one of many ways we can cleanse the mind of pollutants. Laughter is letting go. Laughter—true laughter, laughter that makes us all feel closer as opposed to laughter that makes us feel uneasy and separate—is instantaneous release of anxiety, discouragement, and all other fragmented states. Yet most people think they can only be surprised into laughing. Laughter can be chosen by anyone at anytime. It is truly a "gift of the spirit."

We see in the example of small children that we come into the world naturally exercising the ability to let go through amusement and delight. As I mentioned earlier, little children don't laugh twice as much as adults, they laugh thirty-five times as much! Children are predisposed to laugh. They are pre-amused. Because of this, children can often prevent disturbing thoughts from getting a foothold in their minds in the first place. Under most circumstances, they instinctively shift their preoccupation from a subject of distress to a subject of delight.

Sarah

A few months ago we were with a friend visiting from out of state. He bought a "dream catcher" in a store that sells products made by Native Americans. It looks something like a small round hammock made from a grid of rawhide. Special "cleansing" beads and feathers are attached to the webbing. Placed above your bed, it will catch bad dreams before they can enter your sleep, but it lets the good dreams pass through.

Our friend told us the dream catcher was for his four-year-old daughter Sarah, who for the past several weeks had been having an unusual number of nightmares. The next day our friend flew home, gave the gift to his daughter, and explained how it worked. Sarah's eyes widened as she looked at the colorful dream catcher. She was delighted with the gift and gave her daddy a big hug.

That night, Sarah got out of bed and went into her

parents' room. "Daddy," she said, "I need that dream catcher now." Our friend went into her room and looked around for a place to hang it. A dream catcher is not only supposed to be hung above the dreamer but also in a spot where rays of sunlight will shine on it. The light melts away the trapped bad dreams like fog vanishing before the warmth of the morning sun. Our friend didn't see such a place, but he knew from Sarah's tone that this was an emergency. So he hung it from the ceiling fan—which was neither directly above her nor in line with the light from the window.

When I talked to him several months later, the dream catcher was still on the fan, and Sarah had not had a single nightmare.

The gift her daddy gave her made Sarah happy. Her mind was at war with nightmares, so she dunked it in delight. Typical of a young child, she was willing to substitute happiness for misery.

Many adults would question this approach. They would say, "She never got at what was causing the nightmares." Perhaps in minds as conflicted as ours tend to be, this is an important consideration. But it's also good to see that there are times when we are in pretty good shape mentally—we do have our moments of sanity—and that it isn't always necessary to assume the worst. Rarely do kids of Sarah's age have much hidden stuff, as was shown by the fact that her nightmares never returned.

Once you have identified and disarmed the most destructive aspects of your ego, it is possible to flush from your mind the bits and pieces of rubbish you pick up throughout the day as easily as you turn on the faucet in your kitchen and rinse away some bit of food. Mentally, this process should become habitual, because rarely do we go through a day without picking up something. Above all, the process should be generous. Wash with a flood, not a trickle. Let the shimmering waters of amusement, forgiveness, and letting go flow freely and abundantly throughout your mind. Rinse away petty thoughts, whiny self-criticisms, and debilitating memories in a cascade of release. Do this throughout the day, and especially before you go to sleep.

"I am not amused" is a dominant attitude within most adults—and seemingly for good reason. Let's suppose you have the task of gathering the trash and taking it to the garbage can—fifteen minutes of your life that will not be cited by anyone during your memorial service; fifteen minutes that will not lead to money, fame, improved health, or ecstasy. Obviously, most adults' days are spent in precisely this kind of low-value activity: driving, taking dishes to the kitchen, going to the bathroom, shopping for supplies, dressing, undressing, standing in line, chatting about things they don't really care about with people they don't really love.

There are very few "peak experiences," and in retrospect, these, too, become questionable. The goals and dreams that most people have—even if realized—occupy a tiny fraction of the countless moments of their lives. If achieving fulfillment depends on these fleeting high points, we indeed are doomed to dull and humorless lives. Yet even a brief glance around shows us that precisely this kind of life is the one most people appear to be having. They are not pre-amused about anything because the I-am-not-amused way of looking at life is so deeply ingrained that virtually nothing has a chance of making them smile.

A Righteous Parent

Ironically, I had just finished writing the above paragraph when a man called and said, "Who is this?"

I answered, "I'm Hugh Prather."

He said, "I traced a call that was made from your line."

"What call?" I asked.

"A boy called my home asking for my daughter. I told him she wasn't here, then I asked who was calling. He said, 'Never mind, I'll be seeing her in a hour at the game,' and hung up."

I told the father to hold on and I asked our fifteen-year-old son and his friend if they knew what this was about. It turned out that my son's friend had made the call and had indeed said just about what the man reported.

When I got back on the line and told him that the call had come from our home, he said that he had recorded the call and that I could come over and hear for myself that the boy had not given his name. He said that he didn't know about our home, but in his home this kind of behavior was not tolerated. I asked him if he had ever received another call from our line. He said that was not the point. The point was that we had to teach our children "moral behavior," and he hung up.

Later that evening, when my son and his friend got back from the game, they told me that the girl's father had come to the game and had gotten mad at his daughter for having "friends like that." They said that when the girl's father wasn't around, they told her what had happened. "She was mad that her father had called you," they somewhat gleefully reported.

Teenagers, of course, tend not to leave their names. Some adults don't leave their names. If that small characteristic of human behavior can evoke this kind of confrontation, what chance does this man have of ever experiencing a single day of peace and happiness?

It's worth noting that the behavior itself did not cause anything. Ten other people would have reacted ten different ways. Another father might have taken the call at face value and thought nothing of it. Another might have chalked it up to the adolescent need for secrecy. Another might have begun to wonder who her daughter was meeting at the game. Another might have been relieved that he didn't have to pass on a message. Another might have worried whether this was a burglar checking to see if anyone was home. And so on.

> *Those who think they are superior are at war with all others within their own minds.*

The call didn't *make* him upset; his fractured image of himself did. In his own mind, he was moral and righteous and therefore not a person to be slighted. A thought of superiority or conceit is just one of many polluting thoughts that split the mind. This father's conflicted self-image blocked his intuition and experience. It made him misread the motivation of the boy who called and assume that the boy's intent was to disrespect him. His lack of humor could never safeguard his daughter, and it didn't bring them closer. It didn't even make those of us involved more likely to leave our names. Given the choice to be amused or to be right, he chose to be right, and the only thing he accomplished was to cause isolation and distress, principally within himself.

A Flexible Mom and Dad

Two weeks before this incident, a couple told me they had not been home when their nine-year-old boy had been across the street playing with some other children.

A five-year-old-girl who was part of the group suddenly kicked their son. Reflexively, he hit her in the mouth, causing a loose baby tooth to come out. When the girl's mom and dad rushed outside, what they saw was their little girl crying, bleeding from the mouth, and holding a tooth that the boy, who had now run back across the street, had just knocked out.

Furious, the dad crossed the street, raised the boy in the air by his collar, and shook him. He then dragged the boy back to his side of the street and shouted at him for several minutes.

The couple told me that the first thing they did when they got home and found out what had happened was to carefully sound out their son to see if he was physically and emotionally all right. Then they found themselves getting increasingly angry at the little girl's father. Their impulse was to storm across the street and attack back or, as they said to me, "to try to make themselves feel better by making him feel worse."

This would be most parents' first impulse, including Gayle's and mine. It's interesting that, in situations involving our children, when the desire to attack back is looked at closely, we see that it's mostly indignity at how our child was treated. It isn't truly a desire to improve the situation for the child. It's about us, not our kids. Furthermore, a lack of genuine concern for our kids will always split our minds since any self-absorbed thought is a mental disturbance that includes no unity, no connection.

Somehow this mom and dad were able to stop long enough to ask themselves how could they truly help their boy. First, they let him know that even though he had made a mistake, the girl's father had also made a mistake. In short, they let him know that they were on his side. It then took the three of them over an hour to calm down and quietly consider what they wanted to do next. Eventually, they came up with a plan they all agreed on.

The family crossed the street and rang the doorbell. The mother opened the door, braced for a fight. All they did was tell her how much they loved her little girl, what good neighbors their family had always been, and how deeply sorry they were for what had happened. As they had planned beforehand, they did not bring up what her husband had done.

Suddenly, the mother started crying and she apologized at how her husband had treated the boy. By the time the two families parted, the atmosphere was much improved, and they recently told me it has continued to improve in the two weeks since.

Obviously, the mother's reaction after she opened the door could have been quite different. She could have refused their apology. She could have slammed the door in their face. She could have tried to sue them or involve the police.

This couple had not evoked some kind of universal law that gave them a Kodak moment, they had just tried as best they could to unite their minds around their love for their boy and do what was best for him. In the context of our discussion, they drenched their conflicted minds in peace and consequently were able to act together to defuse what could have grown into a very disturbing situation.

Whether we flood our thoughts with love, stillness, peace, delight, forgiveness, amusement or any other attribute of the Divine, the effect is that the scattered parts of our mind begin coming together, and we can think and act from wholeness.

release 18

Suggested time: 2 or more days)

A. Once or twice today, while you are walking or driving, pick out two points or locations in front of you, one that is near and one that is a little further along. As you approach the first point, say to yourself,

"As I walk from _____ to _____ (this chair to that door, this bedroom to the kitchen), I will look with gentle amusement at everything I see."

"As I drive from _____ to _____ (this utility pole to that stop sign, this parked car to that building), I will look with gentle amusement at everything I see.

B. During the same days that you do A, also single out one or two upcoming errands or tasks. Choose ones that require very little time. Before you start the activity, say to yourself,

"As I _____ (drop by this a store, feed my pet, wash these dishes), I will look with gentle amusement at all that occurs."

If you do A and B even halfheartedly, you will begin to remember what it once was like to look at the world through twinkling eyes.

In practicing being pre-amused:

- Notice that a busy, fractured, or conflicted mindset is temporarily laid aside for a simpler, more peaceful mindset.

- Notice that no matter how many hours or years you have lived within the old mindset, it gives way instantly to your wish to trade it in for peace.

- Notice that your new mindset allows you to see more, not fewer, of the details and nuances of the situation you are in.

- Notice that your new mindset makes you more relaxed about accepting people and situations as they are.

- Notice that when you choose to be gently amused, you are more helpful to yourself and to others without even thinking about it.

Letting Go of "Honesty"

I n discussing the effects of T-thoughts, we have considered several examples of our ability to see and feel what
we believe is present even when it's not. For the sake of
simplicity, I will refer to this as "projection." Since most
of us project unconsciously, we fail to recognize opportunities
to use this mental faculty to our advantage. One such opportunity is in paying attention to which individuals in our lives
we experience as difficult.

Unconscious Projection Feels Honest

All of us know people we find "hard to take," who "push our
buttons," whom we "just can't stand." Those who evoke within
us a strong reaction represent something about ourselves that
we have not made fully conscious. It's actually kind of helpful
to have these people around to remind us that there is still

work to be done. I'm sure you don't believe that, and I don't either, but it's true. Obviously it's not helpful to have individuals around who are a threat to us or our loved ones. No one should endure danger. Nor does it accomplish anything useful to force ourselves to relate to someone who is so disturbing to our family, our business, or ourselves that we can't concentrate. I hope it's also clear that in mentioning people we find difficult, I'm not speaking of the insight we all possess that allows us to see dishonest people as dishonest, conceited people as conceited, or cruel people as cruel. Not every bully is a projection.

I am speaking just of individuals who irritate us personally, who "set us off," who "drive us up the wall." Projection is found in our reaction, which is added to insight. We can perceive that an individual "has a mean streak" without adding condemnation. But if we think, feel, and speak condemnation, we can be certain that we are projecting. The condemnation can feel quite honest, yet this is just one example of the kind of honesty we can do without.

Undoing a projection requires that we see what the people we are reacting to represent in us. What is the importance and symbolism of their behavior? What urges, thoughts, or motives in us are we reminded of? The work before us, therefore, is to see some aspect of our ego that we are presently failing to see, yet "honestly" believe we are seeing within certain individuals.

A simple illustration of this type of unconscious projection is a little boy who spanks his stuffed animals because he himself is spanked. He lectures his elephant, tells it it has been bad, tells it that what he has to do will hurt him more than the elephant. Then he spanks it and says, "No! No! No! No!" At that moment, the boy has no doubt that the elephant is bad. In reality, he unconsciously believes that he is bad.

Other illustrations are a person who brags, but criticizes people who "strut." Or an employee who cheats the company, yet berates those who "don't deserve" the welfare or disability they collect.

Once we uncover the part of ourselves that these individuals are a version of, we do not then reject it. We accept it. We accept that it is an undeniable aspect of our personal ego.

Acceptance in this context means that we admit that we are the way we are. Having done that, now we are in a position to choose not to extend that part of us—but, instead, to extend a deeper, freer, more loving part. Nevertheless, we can't extend what is good about us until we see what we are substituting.

A strong judgmental feeling about someone—especially someone in our life, rather than someone in the news—indicates simple failure to take responsibility for an aspect of our ego. This aspect cannot be guessed or arrived at through reasoning. That won't work. It must be recognized. Yet most people avoid taking responsibility by making this very mistake. For instance, they come up with some reasonable and virtuous-sounding theory about why this person at work irks them. ("She's pretentious and I've never liked pretension"; "He reminds me of my dad, who was nothing but a sweet-talking con man"; "She's truly dangerous to do business with because she acts like a nice person.") As a result, nothing changes.

You will know that you have clearly seen what you were not admitting about yourself when the people who irritate you no longer do—even though they are behaving as usual. You accepted it in yourself, and you accept it in them. In fact, you will feel something akin to affection for them because they have had to deal with the same problem you have.

Using Projection Consciously

Although most people project harmfully—seeing versions of themselves in others and condemning what they see—the following two stories illustrate that projection can be used positively. Even if we are unaware of the mind's capacity to project, it still operates nonetheless, producing effects that we attribute to circumstances, other people, or internal urges that well up unbidden. Whichever way it's used, the ability itself—the mind's power to experience what is not happening—should never be doubted.

Kahuna

Several years ago when I was in Hawaii, I met a woman who was a well-known *kahuna,* or native Hawaiian spiritual healer. She used her ability to see ghosts as a way of blessing homes and businesses. I was so struck by how distinctly she saw various ghosts—she saw two of them while I was with her—and by how harmless she knew them to be, that I realized I could use a version of her approach in my own life.

The particular service she performed was to explain to people that the source of the negative emotions they experienced in their office or home were caused by a ghost. If they could realize that the ghost was harmless and treat it kindly, the source of the negative emotions would be neutralized and their environment would return to harmony. The disharmony, she explained, was caused by misperception. People within the home or office were blaming each other, when all along they were unconsciously reacting to a ghost.

The answer, she said, was not to fight the ghost but to relate to it harmoniously. She suggested simply talking to the ghost—either out loud or silently—in a friendly manner. Perhaps saying, "You have just as much right to be here as I do. I have no ill will against you. Please feel welcome and make yourself at home." Approached in this way, she said, the ghost soon would stop stirring up the atmosphere.

At the time, there was a situation in my life that was definitely inharmonious. So I decided to modify her approach and try it out. There was an old acquaintance I'll call Ralph who was following me around everywhere I went. He would dominate my time after I gave a talk, invite himself to lunch or dinner, and so on. The trouble was that since I had last seen him, he had become disgruntled and very judgmental of everyone and everything.

I "decided" that Ralph was really a ghost and therefore completely harmless. Whenever I was around him, I thought to myself, "Ralph, you are a harmless spirit. You have just as much right to be here as I do. I have no ill will against you. Please feel welcome and make yourself at home."

Seeing Ralph as a judgmental acquaintance, I was annoyed at how he acted. Now, looking at him as a ghost, I was merely curious—because Ralph was the first ghost I had ever seen! This mental game didn't change Ralph, but it made a marked difference in my internal state and in how I reacted to him.

My second application of what might be called "conscious positive projection" (I feel a new book coming on), came a year later when Gayle and I were at a resort town giving a series of workshops. At that same time, two older relatives I'll refer to as Bob and Susan were also visiting the area. For years our contacts with them had been difficult because they were heavy drinkers.

Susan and Bob kept inviting Gayle and me out to dinner, which in itself would have been okay, but because Gayle's dad was no longer around to guide us, as soon as they had a few drinks, they would try to fill his shoes. Consequently, they spent most of our time together criticizing Gayle and giving both of us tips on how to conduct workshops. We didn't react well to this, but we ruled out not seeing them because they were "family."

In discussing how we could handle these encounters more peacefully, we decided to try positive projection. The game that occurred to us was to imagine that we were volunteers for the outpatient program of a nearby mental institution. As part of the program, it was our duty to spend time with the patients they assigned us. Bob and Susan were two such patients. Their mental illness was that they believed whomever they were with were their children. The hospital's instructions were for us to treat them kindly and, whenever they started giving advice or criticizing, to agree with them.

By projecting circumstances and background that were not "honest," we turned these tense dinners into situations that delighted Gayle and me. We would give each other looks across the table whenever the pronouncements started pouring forth, and on the way home we would laugh about how nice we had been in our responses. Bob and Susan also enjoyed the occasions more because Gayle and I agreed with everything they said. And we enjoyed them because we were no longer defensive.

The road to truth is "narrow" in the sense that it is pure, not in the sense that it has limited options.

Letting Go of Rigid Responses
and Limited Answers

Proponents of "honesty" would, perhaps, point out that Gayle and I were dishonest in the above situations. We didn't honor our emotions. We were not true to ourselves. And we didn't "trust" Ralph, Bob, or Susan with the truth. This issue of honesty raises an important question that goes to the heart of what, in my opinion, is a crucial mistake currently being made by many people on spiritual paths, as well as those caught up in the new psychology.

We are all presented with an occasional opportunity to say something, do something, or go somewhere that we know from experience will put us in an unpleasant or even dangerous setting. The classic example is an invitation to a recovering alcoholic to be around individuals who drink heavily. Sometimes, of course, there are work-related occasions that are mandatory, but often a good excuse can get you out of almost anything. Yet many people won't allow themselves this option because of their one-sided definition of honesty

Let's consider what the "honest" answer would be to such an invitation: "No, I won't come because you and your friends get so drunk and boring that I'm afraid I might start drinking again. In case you didn't know it when you hired me, I'm a recovering alcoholic." This may be honest, but it certainly won't lead to greater understanding, deeper friendship, or more job security. It's only half truthful because even though it verbally reflects the mood and opinions of one person, it doesn't give equal consideration to what the other person hears.

The real questions are, Does this brand of honesty lead to increased awareness? Does it inform or does it obscure? If true honesty is an absence of deceit, then the new, popular way of being honest is a path to greater deception.

Today, the ideal of being verbally literal has been raised to religious heights. It is central to separation psychology, which aims to define, distinguish, and "empower" each separated ego. For instance, notice that when people say, "I need to be honest with you," they usually follow with a speech of attack, abandonment, or betrayal.

Occasionally I am asked to counsel an "at-risk" teenage girl who may have a history of falsely accusing people in authority. To put her in a situation where she could be tempted to make this mistake again would not be helpful to her or me. So I always talk to her where other people can see us at all times. But I am not "honest" about this, because she would not benefit from thinking that I didn't trust her. I'll say, "I'd like to get out of this office. Why don't we walk over to the park?" (where there are lots of people).

Today, perhaps the most destructive application of ego honesty is occurring within primary relationships. Many relationships founder before they ever get started because both partners think they must confess every sex act they ever had or thought of having. Note that these confessions lead to greater misunderstanding. They deceive, not enlighten.

Nevertheless, advocates of "honesty" have left no aspect of marriage and family untouched. In the name of openness, partners are supposed to update each other on every negative thought and emotion they have, even though thousands of other thoughts and feelings are not voiced. If husbands or wives have erotic dreams about someone other than their partners, out of the hundreds of things they dream about, these are the ones they must recount. If a parent is contemplating divorce, the kids must be informed because this is "the only honest thing to do." If one parent catches the other parent in an affair, they must "come clean" and tell the children what Dad or Mom did.

Today we try to make our words reflect "how I've been

feeling lately," but we don't ask, "Where within me are these feelings coming from?" We concentrate on making each word a literal reflection of what only part of us is temporarily feeling—yet we ignore other feelings and convictions, as well as how the other person hears our words and what inaccurate conclusions she or he comes to.

The new honesty is about what we say, not about what we communicate, and as such is another version of "appearances are everything." It, like all other aspects of separation psychology, is "all about me" and disregards relationship—our effect on each other.

In Gayle's and my counseling experience, truthfulness is a more helpful concept than honesty. In conversations with the ones you love, be true to your heart instead of honest to your moods. It doesn't even occur to loving parents to be "honest" when their three-year-old brings them a picture and says, "Look what I drew!" They consult their love, their deeper feelings, and say, "That's just wonderful! Let's put it on the refrigerator!" even though they haven't a clue as to what it is. This is truthfulness. The parent is being true to the relationship and true to what the child is really asking.

As can be heard on almost any talk show or read in almost any periodical, we are stuck in a very narrow use of words, and it's not making us happy. Today, language separates rather than joins. It spreads misunderstanding rather than understanding. It gives heat but no real light.

Within ourselves, the choice is always the same: we can come from our connected mind or our separated mind. This is a simple, straightforward choice, yet one that is extremely difficult to make. It is so difficult, in fact, that we get off track daily. When we discover that we have lost contact with our wholeness, sometimes the only thing we can do is merely begin thinking words of wholeness—even though they seem insincere when we start. Words such as "All released; all is

peace." Of course—at that moment—all is not released and
we are not at peace. You can see that strict adherence to the
new honesty-at-all-cost policy would preclude our starting
over in this way.

It should be noted that speaking words of truth to ourselves is not battling negative thoughts with positive thoughts.
In this instance, we are using words to connect with a part of
our mind that we have felt many times before. We are using
words in an attempt to remember. True communication is
remembering that everything is relationship—that, regardless
of the appearance, no one stands alone.

I usually take a walk in the evenings. About once a week my
route takes me down an arroyo where a homeless man has lived
for many years. If he is there at the time, he always walks with
me. Our conversations make no real sense because his mind
crosses seamlessly from reality ("See that rabbit? It's staying
close to us because it knows a coyote is near") to fantasy ("I'll
be moving soon. The professors from M.I.T. have found where
I live, which means the Mafia knows"). But there is an exchange
of warmth, interest, and concern that make these talks as fulfilling as any "intelligent" conversation would be.

During the first two to three years of their kids' lives,
most parents are not tempted to focus on the literal content
of the communications they have with their children. Without
giving it a thought, they see what each exchange is really
about. When diapering infants three to five months old,
bouncing them on their knee, or getting them ready for bed,
there can be wonderful "conversations" between parents and
their children filled with squeals, sputters, gurgles, fast
breathing, and spontaneous bubble blowing. Both parent and
child wave their arms and clap their hands and exchange multiple "ahs" and "ehs." Then perhaps the conversation shifts to
quiet cooing, "ou-ee" singing, and gentle laughter.

Parents would never say that nothing was communicated

between their babies and themselves. Nor would they feel any need to "reflect back" what the child "said" to be certain that the meaning of each syllable was understood.

A parent who has just taken a carton of fresh eggs away from a two-year-old might suddenly hear, "I hate you. I wish you weren't my (mommy, daddy)." But they know what the child is saying—which is not the literal meaning of the words.

Or when young lovers hold each other and gaze up at the stars, the subject of the conversation could be anything, yet both know that the actual communication is, "I love you. I am comfortable with you. I am so happy you are in my life."

The fact is that whenever we talk to someone, two conversations take place. There is of course the subject matter of the words being spoken. But rarely is that where the true importance of the exchange lies for either party.

release 19

Suggested time: 1 or more days

Today, listen to the deeper conversation, the one taking place between your heart and needs and the other person's heart and needs. If you will look into the person's eyes and listen respectfully, you can "hear" quite plainly what this individual is really asking of you. As an aid to doing this, whenever you are engaged in a conversation, slowly (and silently) say to yourself,

"This conversation is about something more than the topic. What is this person really asking of me and what am I truly giving back?"

Instead of being "honest" to the topic, try using the topic merely as a means of having a real exchange, a true connection. Naturally, you don't want to tell the person what they are "really" saying, because that would instantly stop them from saying it. It always breaks our connection with another person to say anything that causes that individual to become defensive or self-conscious. Since feeling our unity with the people around us is in our interest, it is not in our interest to make them withdraw.

Letting Go of the Ego Mind

We have two minds, not just one. Naturally, in order to be believed, this has to be experienced. It's sort of like the notion that we have two stomachs. They never tell you about that in school. They say things like, "There's only one stomach" or, "Only cows have two stomachs" (when, actually, they have four!) or, "When you're full, stop eating." But once you have seen for yourself that, even though you're full, there's always room for sweets—especially chocolate—you begin to suspect.

Then, when you have eaten sweets hundreds of times after you are full, you ask yourself, "Where are these sweets going?" Suddenly you know. We all have a second stomach! One just for sweets. Yet dentists, teachers, first-time parents, and students of "the Chinese healing arts" all want you to stay ignorant of this fact, so they tell you, "Don't eat sugar"—which they know is in everything sweet.

The point is that if you did have a second stomach, the only way you would know about it is to experience it, because no one is going to tell you.

Likewise, the only way we know that we have two minds is to feel the effects of this second mind. Not only do we have a second mind, but once we become familiar with it, we see that the first or ego mind is a kind of fantasy.

Although there has been an occasional reference to two minds, up to this point we have talked mainly about purifying and defragmenting "the mind." Certainly this is an adequate concept that will get the job done. However, many people find it helpful to think of reality as pure and invulnerable. If that is true, there is a part of us—the real part—that remains whole and connected no matter what mistakes we make on an ego level. The mistakes, however, block our awareness of this reality, and it's imperative that we stop making them. We must let go of our unhealed mind if we are to know and be and extend our healed mind.

Saint Paul made a distinction between the "carnal mind" and the "Christ mind," and he said, "Let the mind that was in Christ be in you." Other teachings use terms such as "the Buddha consciousness," "Divine Mind," "the higher self," or "the deeper self" to distinguish the changeless from the changeable, the real from the unreal. Gandhi, for example, taught that we do not somehow make ourselves into truth, but accept truth as it is. In many ways, the concept of "letting go" assumes that the task before us is to be ourselves, not change ourselves. So, if you will indulge me for a moment, let's look at this distinction a little more closely.

For many children, their first friend is imagined; their second friend is real. Only after they have seen the limitations of imaginary friendship do they open themselves completely to friendships that are substantive. Let's say you are a little child and living next door is another little child named Burt whom you really like. Burt has an imaginary playmate named Lubertha. One day you say to Burt, "You think that your only real friend is Lubertha, but some day you'll see that Lubertha doesn't exist. You've made Lubertha up. But I'm real and I'm ready to be a real friend to you. If we can play together just a little, you'll begin to see what I mean."

So Burt begins playing with you—just a little at first. But to do this, he has to let go of his imaginary relationship during the times he spends with you. This is a little scary at first, but soon he sees that he doesn't have anything to be afraid of— you aren't going to hurt him. Then the day finally comes when Burt says, "You know, I think I like real friends best."

Sound too simple? Most things in life are not simple, but attaining a clear, defragmented mind is entirely simple because this second mind—which is your real mind, your deep mind—is already in place, plugged in, and ready to go. If you are like most of us, you have been using your busy, unhappy, fragmented mind for so long that you have merely misplaced your real mind. But you have not lost it. You definitely can work a lifetime trying to shore up a weak, conflicted, hyper active mind. But until you realize that your true mind is the only mind you need, attaining a permanent sense of relax-ation, wholeness, and peace will be difficult.

How the First, or Ego, Mind Forms

Most of us start off being loved for nothing more than being a child. Couples ask themselves, "Should we have a baby?" In their minds, a baby is one thing. When the child comes, it is loved as one undivided whole. Across time and across the world, as parents hold their newborn infants, all they wanted has now been received—for here in their arms is a child.

Yet almost immediately, mothers and fathers begin decon-structing the wholeness of the child. Perhaps it starts with diaper rash, or cradle cap, or a short sleep cycle. Now this part of the child receives more attention than the child as a whole. There is the child's way of sleeping or digesting food, and there are the hundreds of now less relevant features, which become shadows vaguely seen behind the colic or the chronic hiccups. This fragmenting process continues until, finally, only one or two parts of the child are seen at any given time. We no longer have a child; we have a food slinger, or a musical genius, or a bed wetter, or a "C" student.

From our standpoint as children, unless there has been some unusual trauma during gestation or birth, we come into the world feeling and recognizing wholeness. Our minds are simple, united, and focused. We feel one with our parents and want little more than to be near them and have fun with them. Our minds are whole and we are drawn to the part that is still whole within our parents—even if our parents have themselves lost sight of it.

However, we don't remain forever immune to our parents' fragmented way of looking at us. How this failure to love children as a whole affects them is not difficult to see. Most people know at least one or two families in which this dynamic is easily observable. One aspect of the girl or boy is worried over, yet all the while, the overall happiness and well-being of this child is neglected.

Sammy

Several years ago, a mother sought Gayle's and my advice on how to change her four-year-old son's attitude toward his body. Within two years of his birth, Sammy developed a defect that had left one side of his body mildly paralyzed. Although, for her own body, Sammy's mother did not hesitate to use an antibacterial deodorant, disinfecting sprays in her bathroom and kitchen, a germicidal ointment if she cut her finger, a dentist if she had a cavity, or an orthopedist if she broke her leg, she told us that she believed it was a "higher path" to use spiritual means to heal Sammy's body. She said that she knew Sammy's paralysis could be cured if he would simply think of himself as normal, and we soon learned that Sammy's dad agreed with her analysis.

We followed Sammy's progress for three years, which was the time it took us to get his parents to consider taking him to a neurologist, and perhaps more importantly, to relate to him with some degree of enjoyment and appreciation. Yet before this change occurred, Sammy was consistently treated as a failed project, not as a beloved child. He was forced to walk without a crutch, to attempt every sport, and to assume a pleasant, all-is-well affect around his classmates. His parents sincerely thought this approach would benefit him in the long run.

Over the three years, we saw Sammy grow more self-conscious, more frustrated with his own disability, and angrier at almost everyone. In other words, his attitude toward himself and others began to fragment. As the parts of his mind became more separate, they increasingly warred with each other. Separation and conflict are intrinsically linked. Choosing one invariably brings on the other.

Our ego or first mind is at war with almost every image in it. Notice that within its superficial, "idle thought" layer, it is either critical of or wants something from every friend, circumstance, acquaintance, event—and even most strangers! This holds true whether the encounters are in the present, in memories, dreams, fantasies, or thoughts about the future. And, of course, it holds true of its own self-image. On this fractured level, we think that we and everyone else needs to change, at least a little.

Contrast this with most preschool children. Although little kids can definitely become frustrated, note how often they are happy, present, amused, and committed to what they are doing. A happy, amused state of mind is naturally unified and naturally focused. But how infrequently we adults experience this mindset.

In Sammy's case, we shared his parents' belief in the potential of spiritual healing. However, we did not share their thought that a spiritual or strictly mental approach is best for everyone at all times. It is emphatically unhelpful to force this approach on small children, who can't grasp metaphysical concepts.

His mild paralysis, having been separated from Sammy as a whole, became a fixation that created a schism between himself and his parents. They told him that his healing was all up to him. But he was too young to see the flaw in their approach and to defend himself against it.

> *Anything, even a spiritual concept, must be laid aside if it hinders love, for God is love.*

Shortly after his seventh birthday, Sammy's mom and dad flew him across the country to be examined by a team of specialists. They convinced Sammy's parents that his condition was the result of neurological damage and was unaffected by his attitude. The resulting shift in their view of their son was remarkable. Suddenly they withdrew all pressure and began seeking ways to bring comfort and happiness to Sammy within each small task he confronted. Now he was blameless in their eyes and, once again, they were free to love all of him.

Our last contact with this family was when Sammy was nine. At that time his mom and dad were still doing a pretty good job of cherishing their son, although they were beginning to worry a little too much about whether he was "living up to his academic potential."

Although we start out learning the unhappy lesson that we are scattered parts rather than a united whole, a place of wholeness remains untouched within our heart. This is comparable to our state when we dream at night. As we fall asleep, our mind divides into many figures, each with its own agenda. Yet part of the mind remains unaffected by dreams. It keeps us breathing steadily. It stops us from rolling out of bed. It pulls up the covers if we get cold. And so on. In the morning, as we wake to the fact that we are still one self, the mind releases its preoccupation with conflicting dream figures and experiences its wholeness.

However, the power of the mind to believe that its fragmented state is its only reality should not be underestimated. During our period of sleep, we have several clearly defined dreams, many dreamlike fragments, and stages of gradual awakening. Despite the fact that we can be an entirely different figure from one dream to the next and that each dream has its own laws of physics, while we are dreaming we believe in the reality of the dream.

Notice also that when we dream, the mind of the figure who represents us can operate quite differently than the mind we have once we are awake. Not only might our abilities, bodily appearance, and personality be different, but we can, in a sense, have the mind of a different person, with different beliefs, memories, and values—yet still we believe we are who and where we are in that dream.

In the fantasies we have during the day, something similar occurs. Occasionally you can hear one person say to another, "Hey! Where were you? Did you hear what I just said?" What is meant by that is, "Where was your conscious mind when I was trying to talk to you just now?" The person was probably lost in a fantasy.

It should not be surprising that if we can create imaginary playmates and recreate ourselves in dreams and fantasies, we can also create an imaginary identity and believe that it is who we are. In this book, as well as in many religious and mystical systems, this pretend identity is referred to mainly as the ego. Other terms include "worldly identity," "little self," "shadow self," "inner demons," and "separated mind." Our real self (our true, spiritual, eternal self) is a reality so unlike the ego that it cannot be compared or defined.

The imaginary playmate, as is true with each figure in our dreams, has its own motives, thinks its own thoughts, and feels its own feelings. A child can be surprised, even shocked, by what its imagined friend says—even though the child is producing every word. Similarly, the figures in our dreams surprise us, even though we are making them behave as they do. Furthermore, the figures in our dreams, our imaginary playmates, and our imaginary identity or ego defend themselves. Understanding and acknowledging this defensiveness is vital to letting go of the ego part of us.

A dream, for example, will defend itself by creating another dream in which we are waking and getting up, when actually we are still asleep. Or it will incorporate the sound of the alarm or other external disturbance into the dream. When he was four, our son John was knocked out of bed by a 5.7 earthquake, put back in bed, and never woke up. Children who wet their beds often argue that they are not to blame (which, of course, they aren't) because they had a dream that they got out of bed and went to the bathroom. All dreams are set up by the mind to seem real, and so they use mental sleight-of-hand to sustain that illusion.

Likewise, the imaginary playmate defends itself. It might

talk against real friends. It might make an appearance and intrude itself into the ongoing play with another child. Or it might counsel withdrawal, shyness, or seclusion.

Most importantly, our own ego defends itself. It produces a variety of "resistances" to any experience of oneness, love, or connection, which are the essence of our real self or second mind. Each time we know wholeness or even make a small effort to know wholeness, we loosen our grip on our first or ego mind. But having been set up to defend its own sense of reality, our ego always fights back.

For example, notice that whenever you and your partner have a day of closeness and peace, the next day is usually a disaster. Your egos are merely trying to regain the ground they have lost. Of course, if you are vigilant in heeding every attempt your egos make to undo your day of peace, you are immune to those attempts.

The reason you are immune is that the ego is not the devil or "the dark side." It is not an outside force. You produce it, and you maintain it. If you don't want it, you don't have it.

Your first impulse usually comes from your first mind. One instant of stillness, however, takes you into your second mind. It seems like a second or secondary mind because the ego part of us is so dominant and habitual. By going to that place within you where you are whole and connected—your second mind—you automatically begin letting go of your first mind.

> *Your experience of oneness with another is your ego's only enemy.*

By feeling our connection with just one other person, we jump past the boundaries of our imagined separateness. The ego or "autonomous" identity can only be sustained in the mind by constant comparison. This is why another's good fortune diminishes us. We literally feel attacked when, for instance, someone we know comes into a lot of money or receives inordinate praise. And why, likewise, we are buoyed by every sign of weakness and loss experienced by those around us.

How else could our ego—which is our desire to be separate—react? Yet within the experience of love or oneness, we have no need to compare and contrast ourselves with another. We don't need to constantly ask who we are because now we experience it. Worshiping God as a concept will not work. Worshiping God by extending love to others always works.

Letting Go Is "Turning It Over"

Our mind picks up many pollutants during our formative years—during the years that our ego is forming—but the basic fabric of our mind remains pure. Although we may fall into the habit of using our mind in a conflicted manner, no other reality has more basic unity than the mind. Reclaiming our fundamental nature is therefore never a hopeless task. It can be accomplished simply and peacefully, if we take a few small steps each day. The following story illustrates one such step.

Meemo

From the age of six on, and even into my teens, I loved visiting my grandmother, "Meemo." Our basic activity, especially when I was younger, was to play Go Fish and talk about God, although she did manage to sneak in a few lessons on sewing and knitting when my guard was down.

Over the years, I watched Meemo work through several crises, any one of which would have been devastating to most people. Whether it was when her husband died in a plane crash, when her children, one by one, drank themselves to death, or when she developed one of several severe physical problems, she always handled it the same way. I would visit her after a tragedy and she would be a basket case. Then I would go back a week or so later and she would be dramatically better. Although I had seen it all before, I would say, "Meemo, you're doing so much better!" "Yes," she would answer, "I've turned it over to God."

My grandmother never explained what she meant by that, nor did she tell me to use that approach with any of my problems, but I saw her do it for herself so many times over so many years that I began to feel the simplicity and power of the process.

Possibly the reason this particular mental capability is not more widely used is that many people think that it's a function of religious faith. Since they don't have, or possibly don't even want, that kind of faith, they believe the "turning-it-over" capability is unavailable to them.

The faith that God is, that there is Something—a force, a power, a reality, an intelligence, a presence—that understands our questions and inner turmoil and how to lead us out of them, makes relinquishing our problems and emptying our minds of worry far simpler than believing we have to figure out the process alone. This One, this Love, knows the way to us; we do not have to guess, reason out, or somehow stumble across the way to It. For me, it is not a belief but a reality I have experienced countless times—that there is One who leads us all Home. That is my way of describing the experience, but it can be described a thousand other ways.

I also know from counseling hundreds of non-religious people that the ability to "turn it over" is a component of every mind, even the minds of little children. We all have certain mental capacities: the ability to forget, decide, project, remember, concentrate, and so forth. Although these can be used in the name of God, clearly, they also can be used by those who don't use the word *God*. The following story is about a man who had no religious beliefs yet used his ability to "turn it over" to save his life.

Lloyd

One day a man called and told me his friend Lloyd was going to take his own life. He explained that Lloyd had not made up his mind impulsively; it had taken him several weeks to reach this decision. Out of consideration for their friendship, Lloyd had informed him of what he was going to do. The friend had been able to gain one concession: that I could go to Lloyd's home and talk to him.

Although it was midday, I entered a house so dark that I had trouble seeing where I was walking. The drapes were drawn and only one weak light was turned on. Lloyd, a man in his forties, did not get up when I walked in. He was sitting on a couch in the living room, and I pulled up a chair next to him.

Lloyd thanked me for coming, then began explaining why he had decided to commit suicide. He told me the story about how he had lost his job and about how a year or so later his wife had left him, taking their ten-year-old daughter with her. Now she had so poisoned his daughter against him that she no longer would speak to him.

Sometimes people who are suicidal are so withdrawn that finding a way to help them is a guessing game that you are as likely to get wrong as get right. I was fortunate that Lloyd spoke freely. He carefully laid out the case for killing himself.

His family was all that mattered, and now it was destroyed.

As Lloyd talked, I noticed that he kept returning to the same painful memories and characterizations. For example, one scene was of when he had walked out to his wife's car and his daughter wouldn't look at him. One recurring self-evaluation was that he had never been "very likable." As I listened to him, I wrote out a list of these thoughts.

Finally there was a pause, and I said, "I'm not going to try to talk you out of this, but whether you kill yourself in a few hours or a few weeks, there's no need for you to be in this much pain until then. Wouldn't you like to be a little more comfortable and peaceful right now?"

He said that he would, so I went to his kitchen and came back with a plastic wastebasket bag. I tore the list I had made into strips, with one thought per strip, and put them in the bag.

Holding up the bag, I said, "Lloyd, I want you to think of this bag as garbage. To be free of pain, you only have to follow one rule. You can think about any subject in the garbage bag whenever you want, but to do so you must take the strip with that subject on it out of the garbage, and you must hold it in your hands while you think about it. When you feel you are finished, drop the strip back in the garbage."

Luckily, this story has a happy ending. About two years later, Lloyd's friend called me and said that Lloyd couldn't remember if he had ever thanked me for saving his life. Obviously, I had not saved his life. His willingness to do the exercise conscientiously had saved it.

The act of consciously picking a thought up and consciously putting it down allowed Lloyd to experience moments of freedom. He saw that his feelings of desolation faded without a line of thinking to drive them, yet quickly returned when he used his mind in the old way. As he said in a conversation we had later, "I realized that I am the only authority on what can hurt me."

> Never worry whether you know the correct way to pray, seek guidance, or ask for help. When the request for peace comes from the heart, a way to have peace is always provided.

To let go of his suicidal impulse, Lloyd had to be aware of his disturbed, or in his case, self-destructive, feelings. Since he kept his house dark, had openly acknowledge his suicidal intent, and had agreed to allow someone to try to help him, Lloyd was clearly aware of his feelings. However, even in cases of suicide, this is not always a given. Some people impulsively kill themselves when only moments earlier they didn't recognize that they were in such dangerous emotional straits. This is also true of some individuals who murder or batter impulsively.

However, these are exceptions. Very few individuals have no awareness of their emotions before acting destructively. Unacknowledged feelings are no longer the block to mental wholeness they were a few decades ago. Ironically, we are now overly aware and indeed fixated on our emotions, and this has become a new impasse. Fortunately, this impasse is not difficult to get beyond once we identify the thoughts behind our emotions. By doing this we give ourselves the option of releasing both thought and feeling.

Learning a process whereby we "switch channels" from our superficial layer of thoughts to our deeper, more peaceful layer, from our first mind to our second mind, is important to our success. It simply does us no good to turn it over to God, or turn it over in any other way, if we remain unaware of what needs to be turned over.

In the early stages of our journey toward wholeness, we vastly underestimate the number of destructive ways we use our minds. Many things we do mentally that we believe benefit us, or do us no real harm, are later seen as abhorrent—for instance, judgments we indulge about our partner or our child. Eventually, each misuse of the mind has to be acknowledged as an actual misuse.

For example, to say to ourselves, "I will have no more idle thoughts," or, "I will have no more ego," may not at first appear to be a misuse of our mind. But its effect is to throw most of us into deeper confusion and chaos. We merely split our mind, with parts of it pitted in judgment against other parts. Conflict is the outcome.

This mistake is similar to a child trying to order his or her imaginary playmate out of the room, or yelling at it to shut up. Confrontation makes the imaginary playmate seem all the more real, since it won't cooperate. Similarly, we should never battle our ego because it's merely what we still want. Again and again we must clarify what we do want until, at last, all our wanting is unconflicted.

Letting Go of Scattered Thinking

Awakening is not dying, or going somewhere else, or attaining an exalted spiritual state. When the presence of the Divine is more dominant in our experience than the presence of chaos, we are awake. For most of us, this is a gradual process. As we increasingly think and act from the part us that is still, gentle, and deeply connected to all things, it is as if this part expands. Our thoughts are more natural, our perceptions more comforting, our actions less jolting to ourselves and others, and we feel and become increasingly real.

As this process continues, a remarkable thing happens. Even the picture of separation that surrounds us begins to reflect the oneness and comfort of the Divine. People and worldly events do not necessarily change. Our life story doesn't suddenly take on some charmed and magical quality. Although the picture before us is the same, now it holds a great pleasure instead of a curse. It is softer to the eyes and gentler to the ears. The experience of Home begins to anoint us.

As you proceed in the ways we have been discussing, you will be increasingly aware of whether your thoughts are scattered or whole, or to put this in terms of two minds, whether you are in your first mind or second mind. Simply noticing this much is a modest goal that keeps before you a clear choice: Do I want to know innocence or guilt, happiness or fear, unity or loneliness, flexibility or rigidity, the peace of God or the chaos of the ego? Seeing that you want wholeness, the only question remaining will be, "Am I ready to choose wholeness this instant—within *this* situation, during *this* activity, in the face of *this* problem, task, tragedy, or minor distraction?"

Binkley and Mousse

That most powerful of all human forces—the mind of a two-year-old—proves what a single focus, exercised in the present, can accomplish. Two-year-olds win the battle of wills with their parents over and over because they are focused and they stay focused, whereas parents have multiple goals and don't stick to a single objective more than a few moments.

We have a cat named Binkley who is almost as mentally powerful as a two-year-old. Binkley simply can't be distracted. When Gayle rescued him from a college dorm three months ago and brought him to our home, Binkley immediately set out to make our dog Mousse play with him. But Mousse would have nothing to do with such an unnatural relationship.

First, she used her fierce bark and growl to keep Binkley at bay. When that didn't quell Binkley's interest, she tried adding terrifying lunges. This too failed: Binkley merely moved to high surfaces and would playfully bat Mousse from above.

Last week, Binkley finally got the breakthrough he had been seeking. Lying several feet away from Mousse, time and again he stretched out his paw and gently touched Mousse's paw. By now, she knew that running after him was pointless because he was too fast for her. So each time she was touched, she would jump up and spin around in the air, hoping sudden movement would put an end to this nonsense. But finally, Mousse got interested in the game and put her nose where Binkley could touch it. From that point, it was inevitable that gently mouthing Binkley's paw would follow. Mousse's heart now belonged to Binkley.

Most adults scatter their chances of fulfillment over the past, present, and future and are surprised that little kids outendure them and get what they want. Adults are conflicted. Kids are not. Even ideas that can unite people's minds around a political, school, or neighborhood issue, or ideas that can call a nation to war, never last. Once a better ally, a hotter issue, or a more formidable enemy comes along, the feelings of unity evaporate surprisingly quickly. Only a spiritual idea can unite the mind permanently, because it alone is based on truth that lasts.

Jordan

Our son Jordan took up tennis when he was twelve. He worked hard, had good teachers, and progressed rapidly. One day, Mark, his regular pro, had to cancel, and I arranged for a pro named Benny to give the lesson. Benny's teaching aim for the day was for Jordan to hit thirty consecutive shots without putting one in the net. This was a difficult goal for a boy who had only been playing a couple of months. But Jordan had proven himself to be a fast learner, so as he went through his first series of thirty, Benny made suggestions and pointed out mistakes each time Jordan's ball hit the net.

This continued for almost half an hour. Although Benny's instruction helped, Jordan was never able to hit thirty balls without netting at least five.

Finally Benny stopped the drill and walked over to his own racquet bag and pulled out a bill. He said, "Jordan, this could be a hundred dollars. I have been known to use that much." He put the bill on the service line (which is about halfway from the net to the back line) and set a ball can on top of it. Then he said, "If you can hit the next thirty balls past the service line but inside the baseline—and not hit one ball in the net—I'll give you the bill that's under this can." This was an even harder task than the first drill, because, before, he had not had to hit past the service line.

Without any further instruction, Jordan hit the next thirty without a mistake. Benny then picked up the bill and walked over to Jordan. "As you can see," he said, "this is only a dollar. So don't think you did that drill perfectly for a lot of money. You succeeded because you had a single goal." He then pulled a twenty out of his bag and gave it to Jordan.

Turning a problem over to God is an example of a single spiritual idea that unites the mind. Benny was teaching tennis, not an approach to life. "You get the bill if you don't hit the net" is a goal that can unite a mind for a few minutes only. With another kid on another day, it might have had the opposite effect, increasing pressure and lowering performance skills. I never saw Benny use that approach with Jordan again because he knew that it probably wouldn't work a second time.

Yet the concept of "turning it over to God" had the power to unite my grandmother's mind for a lifetime. It was an idea that pointed to the Divine and nothing else. *Using* that idea—interrupting irrelevant focuses and returning to that one focus—was my grandmother's way of letting go.

Letting Go of Blame and Damage

We tend to think of a problem as a specific situation, person, or condition, when the actual difficulty is our belief that something outside our heart must change before our heart can change. No matter what form it takes, this belief blocks our freedom.

Guilty Builder, Guilty House

Gayle and I bought the house our family now lives in while it was still under construction. It has several double doors, and shortly after we moved in we noticed that they had not been hung properly. Each set of doors leans together at the top, thereby providing roomy corridors at floor level through which insects can enter our home at their leisure.

Insects love Tucson. They appreciate the mild winters. Since there is so little ground vegetation in the desert, they have an unobstructed view of the mountains. However, within the bug population there are some very bad characters and periodically (about once a week) we had to ferret these out and remove them from our home.

We told the builder about the problem, and on several occasions showed him the gaps. He always assured us that he had ordered the necessary parts from the door manufacturer, who, he said, had failed to supply him in the first place. But somehow the parts never came in. Year after year went by. Neighborhood insects told their friends about the Prather Insect Resort and the crowds grew. Gayle and I did our part to keep the doors wide open by complaining to each other and our friends about the builder's irresponsible behavior.

Four years went by before we faced the fact that the builder wasn't going to act. We then made a few phone calls, asked a few questions, and ended up buying some sticky felt pads, the kind that are available in any hardware store. In two hours we corrected the insect problem.

We asked each other why we hadn't done this sooner. True, we wanted the builder to rehang the doors, but the insects could have been stopped the day after we moved in. The fact was that it hadn't even occurred to us to do something ourselves—because it was the builder's responsibility! As you may have noticed, in our culture "responsibility" has come to mean "guilt." "The builder should take responsibility" really means "the builder should admit he's guilty." Naturally, the builder was saying, "The manufacturer should admit he is guilty."

The simple fact was that we hadn't corrected the insect problem because the insect problem proved the builder's continuing guilt. We wanted proof of guilt more than we wanted freedom from insects.

And *we* teach this stuff!

As often as Gayle and I have worked to release ourselves, our children, and other loved ones from the past, our own house was a big blind spot. In the year since seeing this, we have expanded what might be called our "blessings of release" to include not only our house, but our dog, cats, plants, car, pieces of furniture, and any other part of our life that may be dragging some bit of unpleasant history behind it.

There are individuals and families who have a bond with their house or apartment. They love it and care for it as if it were a cherished pet or child. Their dwelling gives back a warmth that welcomes them home and provides a haven from the world. Occasionally visitors sense this bond and say, "This place has such a wonderful feeling."

Although it makes sense in relationships between human and animal, I frankly don't know how it's possible that inanimate objects can give back warmth. But certainly the opposite is also true. There are places with very dark, disturbed, or depressed atmospheres. This is so universally recognized that some states require that potential buyers be informed that, for example, a murder was committed in the house for sale.

Although I don't understand how a home, car, or large plant can seem quite human, I do know one way it is brought about. If in your heart you say to your pet, garden, or house, "I know what happened to you before, but that is not happening to you now. I release you from your history. Now you are my (dog, tree, kitchen), and I am responsible for how I treat you and think about you. My choice is to think of you kindly, and I am determined to be consistent about this."

So there you are outside tending your garden, and now the water you spray is a shower of blessing, the branches you prune are gentle health care, and the weeds you pull are sheer beautification. Somehow your attitude embeds itself deep in the tissue of the garden. Just ask those who love to water and tend their gardens.

Letting Go of Body Thoughts

More important than the bond we form with our garden or our home is the potential bond we could form with our body. When I mention this thought to people on metaphysical and spiritual paths, they sometimes raise the objection that the body is not real, or the body is a false sense of self, or the body is the source of our lower or primal urges.

It's curious that no one questions the thought that we can love, care for, and identify with flowers, trees, birds, and other little creatures of a garden. People even tell stories of heart-to-heart talks they had with ants that staked out their kitchen. No one questions blessing a house and feeling blessed in return. In fact, many people have house-blessing ceremonies and give "housewarming" gifts. But the body, our most immediate and constant habitat, is somehow different.

It is so different that most of us are in constant battle with our hair, teeth, skin, toenails, fat cells, the length of our nose, and our overall height, shape, and age. These battles become more fearsome the deeper into the body we look: pesky sinuses, misbehaving bowels, falling arches, painful backs, unreliable knees, and achy joints. Then of course there are the life and death struggles with our vital organs, immune systems, nervous systems, and blood chemistry. I could go on, but it becomes a horror story.

In short, most people fear and distrust their body, feel betrayed by it, and at times hate it. In typical fashion, our solution is to ignore this relationship and simply allow our hidden fears and resentments to fester.

This is not necessary. We can let go of disturbing body thoughts just as we can any other disturbing thought, and we must do this if we are ever to know our peaceful mind. Maybe you have seen people come to peace with their bodies as they were dying, but why wait until then?

Suggested time: 1 day

A. Take off your clothes and stand in front of a mirror, a full-length one if possible.

Notice how hard it is just to do this much. What are your emotions? Fear of what you will see? Guilt? Embarrassment? Is your mind racing around trying to think why this suggestion is mistaken, bad, or dangerous? Most of us have gotten ourselves into such a mental mess that just looking at the body is this big an issue. A little child would follow this suggestion without hesitation. It can't be the chore of taking off the clothes. We do that every day to bathe or shower and don't give it a thought. Try to identify exactly what it is that makes you give it a thought *this* time. What precisely are the thoughts that make up this resistance? Remember, these are thoughts you have been lugging around for a long time.

B. Beginning with the top of your head, next go to your forehead, then your eyebrows, your eyes, and so on through to your toes. First, stare at your hair (or bald head) and continue staring until your mind becomes quiet. (If it helps, you might say something like, "This is simply hair. It's the hair I have today. I don't have the hair I had ten years ago. Most people have hair; this happens to be mine.") As you stare, be aware of any judgments, anxieties, bad associations, or any other negative beliefs or opinions you have about your hair. Speak them out loud if this will help identify the thoughts.

C. Then say to yourself, "These are my thoughts. Do I want to carry around all these thoughts about my hair?"

D. Repeat B and C with the other parts of your body.

E. Having now uncovered the disturbing and separating thoughts about your body, starting again at the top of your head and going down your body as before, call on your thoughts of gratitude and appreciation about each part you look at. ("Thank you, hair, for keeping me warm, for putting up with my curses and sighs, for patiently tolerating all the chemicals I mindlessly dump on you. . ." "Thank you, forehead, for protecting my brain, for showing concern or surprise as needed. . ." "Thank you eyebrows, for keeping the water out of my eyes, for giving me that certain heavy-browed look. . . .")

You want to *sincerely* see how much your body has undergone for you; how in so many ways it has been a good friend; how innocent it is of the genes it inherited, the climates it has endured, the accidents it has sustained, and all the other external forces like gravitation and sun rays that changed it in ways it could not help. In other words, you have real cause to feel affection for your body and to treat it gently. It means you no harm. It has done the best it could. It has been as faithful as any pet, and it is as closely related to you as any "biological child."

Why, then, single out this one object among so many to say, "It's not spiritual to think about"? To feel a bond with anything in your life cannot hurt you spiritually. If a garden or a house can reflect back warmth, certainly the body can as well.

F. Resolve now that from this time on you will treat your body gently, talk to it kindly, and above all think of it happily.

Letting Go of T-Thoughts

In this book we have explored several ways that polluting thoughts can be removed and our minds made whole. To put it in the context of this chapter, ways that we can switch from our first mind to our second mind. Before the mind can be unified—or we can "put on" our unified mind—our deep resistance to that transition must be removed. We have identified the primary source of our resistance as our T-thoughts, and we have searched for, looked at, and worked to release these in several ways. There is still one important aspect of T-thoughts that I have not emphasized: their promise and appeal.

All T-thoughts are like a plant with dark roots of chaos and green shoots of promise. Only by clearly seeing both does our willingness to release these thoughts become strong.

The *roots* extend into the past—which includes the history of this thought's effects on us and the other people in our life as well as the roots' origin in the dynamics of our home life as a child.

The *green shoots* of promise include benefits we think we receive from maintaining our belief in the thought. These feelings are sometimes particularly unpleasant to acknowledge because of what they say about us.

Let's say you're listening to your husband talk about how nice it would be to own a boat. Suddenly you are flooded with angry thoughts of how untrustworthy, even dangerous, your husband is. How could he even think of spending that kind of money when the two of you just finished discussing your credit card debt?

You now have several options:

- You can yell at your husband, but then he would yell back, and soon you would be locked in another long fight.

- You can demand to know how he could think of buying a boat at a time like this, but he might cover his tracks by saying he wasn't thinking of buying one.

- You can start silently repeating, "God will protect me from my husband. God will protect me from my husband. . . ." Or, "My husband is really a good person at heart. My husband is really a good person at heart. . . ."

- OR–you can look closely at the thought itself.

You begin with the dark roots of the thought. For instance, maybe you ask yourself, "Where does my belief that my husband is dangerous come from?" Perhaps you start by considering his past actions. You ask yourself if his patterns lead you to believe that he will buy a boat behind your back. After considering this honestly, you see that you really don't think it's likely that he will.

Tracing the roots further back, the next thing you see is that you have often looked down on your husband's tendency to daydream. He is always building air castles and hoping for magic. However, after closely examining this characteristic, you see that his dreams and visions are actually part of what you love about him. What you really object to is the absent-mindedness this dreaming causes. Absentmindedness often prevents him from hearing you and recognizing your needs. Yet, failure to see other people's needs is a fault you have often criticized in yourself. Perhaps you are seeing a version of yourself in him. You decide to watch your thoughts more closely when your husband becomes absentminded.

As you continue to explore the question of where your belief that your husband is dangerous comes from, you begin to connect it to a story you heard while growing up. When you were too young to remember, your family lost everything when your father went bankrupt. The tales of what happened as a result permeated your childhood. Perhaps you are angry at your dad and need to forgive him.

The notion that you could be angry for losing a lifestyle you never experienced seems very unlikely, yet something has been making you overreact to money issues. You decide that it could do you no harm to hold your dad in light and to continue doing so until you know with all your heart that you have forgiven him.

Next, you ask yourself what effect distrusting your husband has on you physically. Immediately you notice that you are more anxious, that your stomach feels a little sick, and that there is tension in your shoulders.

Then you ask what impact has your distrust had on your marriage and your relationship with your children.

And so on, until you feel that you have seen the complete root system of this distrust.

Turning your attention now to the green shoots of promise, you ask what rewards, benefits, and payoffs you get from continuing to distrust your husband.

First you see that you believe this attitude will protect you financially. Yet on further consideration, you acknowledge that your past displays of distrust have sometimes made your husband so angry that he did things you didn't like, some of them financial.

As you look closely at your emotions during your displays of distrust, you notice that one of them is a feeling of excitement. One part of you is actually glad when he does something untrustworthy. What is that all about? You decide to watch this feeling carefully in the future to see if it indicates a desire to have proof of your husband's financial irresponsibility or of your superiority, or maybe that now he "owes you one," or even that this gives you a get-out-of-marriage-free card. You will wait to see rather than guess.

Next you ask yourself if your distrust gives you any leverage in your marriage. For example, does it give you an advantage during an argument? Or does it make it more likely you will get your way when you make certain demands? And so on.

At the end of your examination of this distrust thought— which, if it is chronic, could take many hours or even weeks— perhaps you see that you don't believe that your husband is truly a financial threat to the family. You see that the distrust indicates that a deep commitment to forgive your dad is essential. You also see that distrusting your husband damages a partnership that means everything to you, more even than credit card debt.

Now the thought is actually disarmed rather than just hammered into the unconscious through "positive" thinking. All that is left is for you to take a firm, consistent stand on your love and appreciation of your husband. Here's how that works:

- Your T-thought will surface again and again because it is a foundational part of your particular ego.
  However, if you have done your awareness work thoroughly, the T-thought will no longer scare you, confuse you, or upset you. You will feel no urge to resist it, argue against it, or replace it. And if you have *really* done your awareness work, you will find your T-thought quite funny.

There is no way to perfect egos. Nor is there any reason to. Why would you want to perfect an imaginary playmate? Would that get rid of it?

> *Certainly not. Likewise, there is no need to make a project of your ego and attempt to perfect an imaginary identity. Just seeing it clearly will show you that you don't want it; don't need it; and don't have to fear it.*

- Whenever your T-thought surfaces, just look at it long enough to identify it. Then ask yourself, "Do I want to hurt (whoever is the target of the thought) by acting on this thought?"

In asking that question, you plug into your true feelings, your true mind. You will *feel* your compassion for this person and you will *know* that you wish no harm. Now the thought is dismissed.

- If on some occasions you are so angry at the person that the honest answer is that you *do* want to hurt him, then ask yourself if this T-thought is the part of you that you wish to extend, nourish, and have grow. If you have seen your T-thought clearly, you will feel no hesitancy in your response. You emphatically do not want that part of you to grow and you will not act it out. Now the thought is dismissed.

I must tell you that all of this does not usually work quite this neatly in practice. Realistically, you will not be perfectly thorough in looking at your T-thought, and you *will* be somewhat fearful or confused when this thought surfaces. This confusion can last many weeks or months, depending on how deeply rooted the thought is. Nevertheless, each time you see your T-thought and refuse to act on it, you decrease your fear of it. This more gradual process is perhaps the most common way that T-thoughts are eventually released.

However, once you have identified a T-thought and have seen how much harm it has caused you and others, if you consciously choose to act it out again and again, it will grow enormously in power. Seeing how we have damaged ourselves and the ones we love eliminates our option to continue doing so. You can't indulge your desire to harm "just a little" without paying the price of a surprisingly large setback.

By this point in the book, if you have been doing the Releases, you should have a clear idea of one or two of your T-thoughts. At the heart of most of these is a deep unforgiveness or fear. If this is true for you, the following guided meditation is an additional way of releasing grudges, grievances, or bitterness, which tend to be the most persistent thoughts that any of us carry around. Naturally, this meditation can be used in whole or in part whenever the need arises.

release 21

Suggested time: 1 or more days

- Choose a person about whom you often think painfully, angrily, or defensively. Picture this person standing before you now. Make him or her as "real" as you can by imagining the way this person usually dresses, stands, gestures, and the like.

As you look this individual over, recall the negative things he or she has done and the weak or destructive characteristics this person possesses. Be sure to include any slight or betrayal or anything else negative that was done to you personally.

- Now, instead of fighting, judging, or pushing down your negative thoughts, first give them full rein so you can see them clearly. Ask your ego what it would like to do or have happen to this person. Search out any "justice" or payback fantasies you have. Say to this person, "What you deserve is. . . ." Or, "If it were up to me you would. . . ." Be as detailed as you can about all punishments this person's weakness, self-pity, treachery, deviousness, or cruelty deserve. If you can expand on your revenge fantasies until they become funny, this is best. If that isn't possible, keep elaborating on them until you reach a sense that you have thoroughly explored your feelings.

- Look once again at this person, and continue looking until your focus is calm and steady. Now see Jesus— or whatever other figure represents love, peace, or the Divine to you—standing behind this person. Watch as Jesus, or whomever you have chosen, walks into this individual.

- Continue to look at this scene, and witness the brilliant light of the Divine shining so brightly from within this person's heart and being that soon there is nothing present but the light.

- End by setting a single purpose. From this point on, your goal is to think about this individual in peace. It is *not* to like or understand this person. Nor is it to make the person fond of you. It is simply to remain at peace whenever this one individual comes to mind.

release 22

Suggested time: 1 or more days

We all nurture and exercise our misery with countless little thoughts throughout the day. Yet all we need is to be aware of how and when we do this, and the door to freedom swings open.

As an aid to accomplishing this, let me suggest the following line of thought:

"I will practice noticing just this much today: I alone choose what ruins my attitude and complicates my life. I live with the decisions I make about everything and everyone around me. I move among these decisions. They mean the world to me. An overcast day is nothing more than an overcast day until I decide what it withholds from me personally and pick what mood it must inflict. A little extra money is just a little extra money until I decide I must show signs of having it. A tailgater is just a tailgater until I make him my personal nemesis and seat a grievance beside me. My teenager is merely a child until I paint her as 'manipulative.' Now my mental home is decorated in the same unhappy hue."

Today, take note of any personal conclusion you trip over and of every predisposition you stumble into. Today, hold to one simple idea:

"I see what I decide and react as I choose."

Letting Go of
"Spiritual" Specialness

Within the eternal changeless nature of Truth, we are not our busy, fractured minds. Yet it is crucial to acknowledge that we believe we are indeed fractured. Every day we accept our ego thoughts and feelings as our only thoughts and feelings.

Even though our ego represents the conflicted voices and lessons we stockpiled during our formative years, we react to them as our essence, our individuality, how we "feel" about things. If we are honest, we will admit that this part of us is our primary teacher and guide. We are not on a spiritual path; we are on an ego path.

Letting Go of Spiritual Attainment

Obviously, we can have the *concept* that we are not our ego (our inner demons, shadow self, mortal self, dreaming mind, busy mind), but in a thousand ways each day, we demonstrate that we live through and for our worldly identity.

You and I do not *believe* we are "children of God." We may give lip service to that concept, but we believe we are autonomous, a creation of ourselves. We think we are pretty much whatever we decide to be and not the creation, the extension, the "image and likeness" of God. This belief is not "nothing." It creates almost everything we experience. It is the source of our fear, misery, and loneliness. It locks us in a tale that begins with hope and excitement, but ends in disillusionment and destruction. It doesn't matter if this tale is not the truth of God, because you and I experience it as if it were.

When we are in a restaurant, we look over the menu and select a dish. We don't think, "Oh, this preference for linguini is coming from my ego and is not my preference." We order the linguini. Without any real second thought, we accept almost every reaction we have to the circumstances and people we encounter each day—even though only our ego has a range of emotional responses to aspects of separation. Surely no one would argue that God likes fried okra over lima beans. No one would say that the governing Principle of the universe hates "call waiting." Or suggest that the Host of Heaven "buy American."

From the array of emotions within them, individuals on a spiritual path often single out just a few feelings and call them "ego." For instance, we can "love" getting a promotion and feel euphoric for a day or two, yet not have an instant's concern that these are ego reactions. But if we feel jealousy about someone else getting the promotion and we are depressed for day or two, we say, "These emotions are my ego." Or if it dawns on us that we dislike the French, or yuppies, or our brother-in-law, we think, "That's just ego."

From thirty years of counseling individuals on a spiritual path, I know that when most people say, "That's just ego," or, "That's my inner parent," or, "That's the devil," or, "That's just the alcohol talking," what they really mean is, *it is not me*. And, of course, from the standpoint of absolute Truth, it isn't. Yet notice that it is them when it comes to the opinions they hold about politics, religion, parenting, or whether they are "good in bed."

In fact, we tend to be proud of most of our patterns of separation: "I'm a morning person," "I run a tight ship," "I believe in speaking my mind," "I don't tolerate fools," "I'm a spontaneous kind of guy," "When I pay this much, I expect good service."

I can't emphasize too strongly that we run the risk of underestimating the power of our beliefs when we notice a destructive line of thought but say to ourselves, "Oh, that's just ego." Our beliefs are so powerful that they color our entire world. We literally see what we believe, but we can and most of us do—fail to take responsibility for what we see, especially, what we see within. Provided it's not acted out, consciously blaming others for how we feel is a fairly obvious and innocuous mistake compared to the mistake of attributing our feelings to the ego or the devil.

Obviously, there is nothing wrong with using the word *ego* or terms like *dark impulses, inner demons,* or *shadow side.* The danger is believing that once we have identified the impulse as ego, we have accomplished something. Far better to think, "I have destructive sexual impulses," or, "My fears about money are of no benefit to anyone"—than it is to plead with God to destroy them or to dismiss them as if we didn't choose them.

When we enlist our spiritual beliefs or the power
of our will to do battle with our darker impulses,
we start pumping new life into them.

Attributing our harmful tendencies to something that is "not us" tempts us to stop taking the steps needed to render them powerless. To reiterate what I said earlier, once any destructive thought is made fully conscious, we still recognize it whenever it surfaces, but it no longer scares, shocks, or controls us. As a safety precaution, Gayle and I counsel people to think, "I hate women," "I disdain men," "I feel superior to my best friend," "I can't stand three-wheelers," "I resent mansions," rather than, "My ego is feeling hateful (disdainful, superior, resentful, and the like)." We purify ourselves by acknowledging how we are now and becoming more aware of it now.

Little situations arise almost daily that disturb us. A driver honks; a friend criticizes; we discover termites; someone neglects to thank us; and so forth. Then what happens? We recognize that we are embarrassed, resentful, anxious, offended—and think we shouldn't feel that way. If we were further along spiritually, we say to ourselves, we would just shrug it off. Now our mind starts shuttling between revising the scene to our advantage and perhaps having a "payback" fantasy or two, and on the other hand, disliking the fact that we are obviously upset. We think, "What mistake am I making that causes these feelings?" Then we try to destroy the feelings with scriptural texts, mantras, or "common sense," as if pure ideas on top of impure ideas make a clean mind.

Our desire to look away from our petty impulses
is not a desire for more oneness, equality, or love.
The reality that many people would be upset by

> *what just upset us makes us uneasy. The fact*
> *that it happens to many drives us to resist it*
> *happening to us. In short, we don't want to be*
> *ordinary. We are among the chosen few who do*
> *not get upset. Where is the oneness and equality*
> *in that?*

We further complicate our task by encouraging each other to believe that if we could just come up with the right interpretation, we wouldn't feel this way. For instance, we tell stories about how some perception-changing bit of information immediately made someone feel more forgiving: "The waiter snapped at her but a few minutes later she found out that his wife and eight children had just died leaping from a burning building."

Maybe the waiter is rude because the waiter is a rude person. There are, after all, people who are rude, dishonest, sadistic, and murderous. No one who gets stung by an ant asks how does this fit into the Divine Plan. No one seeks to understand the motive of an angry moose. Ants sting; moose are grumpy; we forgive them both.

Then there are those of us who smugly tell other people things like, "Whenever I feel judgmental, I just tell myself that the person (probably had alcoholic parents; probably is unhappy in love; probably needs a break; probably has low blood sugar from not eating.)" Translation: "*You* may have trouble being judgmental, but *I* have a simple remedy." Indeed, it's judgment that prompts such a statement.

> *If we could just see that we all make pretty*
> *much the same mistakes, maybe we would*
> *lighten up on each other. But I doubt it.*

It's not that any of the above approaches couldn't work if someone saw the value of forgiveness and truly wanted to *be* forgiving. Yet most people really want to make other people guilty and they jumble their mind by frantically searching for the magic thought that will make that impulse unconscious.

If we ask ourselves, "How *do* I react to what just happened?", our mind now has a chance to see our upset honestly and pass through it to a deeper layer of thoughts. But if we say, "I don't want these thoughts"—which really means, "I want to be spiritually special"—our mind pulls away from our ego like a hand pulling away from a hot surface, and we never have a chance to move past this superficial layer to our core. It's better to *run* with the thoughts, to embellish our ill will, to plumb the depths of our outrage—and to do this until we see that we are no better than anyone else. Now we aren't afraid to be normal and equal and can experience oneness directly.

However, normal doesn't mean thinking of ourself as a "guilty sinner." We are in danger of self-deception if we believe that once we have shamed ourselves by admitting our failings, we have begun to change for the better. We have not. Taking responsibility for our darker impulses does not call for guilt. Guilt is just another form of separateness and being special. Instead of thinking we're better than others, we think we are worse—but we don't think we are equal and connected.

To lecture and disrespect ourselves as a way of combating destructive impulses keeps us from taking responsibility for our unhealed mind. Valuing attack is valuing attack, regardless whether someone else or we ourselves are the object of the attack. It's insane to think that because we can catalog our mistakes, we therefore see ourselves more clearly than God sees us. You and I eventually will come to know and embrace our God-given innocence, as will everyone. Telling ourselves that we were so damaged by childhood or are so inherently corrupt that we personally will never reach that point merely invests words with magical qualities and denies the power of our own choices.

Letting Go of a "Higher" Path

In the last few years, Gayle and I have come to what was for us an unexpected conclusion. Although we ourselves are ministers, we now doubt the value of a spiritual path, almost any spiritual path, *as it is usually practiced.* In our opinion, if your purpose is to experience your oneness with God, to be of true help and comfort to the people around you, and to have a growing sense of peace and unity, a religious, metaphysical, or spiritual approach to life often works against these goals. It doesn't have to be this way, but it usually is.

"Everyone is on a path," many openly devout people say. But what they seem to be thinking is, "I, however, am on a *spiritual* path." In other words, "Now that I believe in oneness, I see that you and I are not one."

From having repeatedly fallen into this trap myself, I now realize that nothing is more selfish or separating than thinking that you, personally, have a higher approach to life than other people. It's ironic that individuals with strong spiritual beliefs often have larger egos, are more rigid, are more unconsciously judgmental, and are more uncomfortable to be around than people who have little interest in pursuing mystical, religious, or metaphysical teachings. Those who assume the mantle of oneness often lack the desire to *experience* oneness with anyone.

The ego part of us does not act independently of our wishes, because it *is* us—at least that is our evident and deeply held conviction. If we are still judgmental of our teenager, we still want to be judgmental of our teenager. If we are still confused about what our partner wants from us, we still want to be confused. Obviously, believing in oneness doesn't automatically decrease the desire for oneness, and many people both believe in it and practice it. Yet it's interesting how often we trumpet what we ourselves fail to do and criticize in others what we ourselves do regularly.

> *Have you noticed that most people who say, "I've finally learned to say no," never had much trouble saying it in the first place?*

When good people devote themselves to a good teaching, how could the outcome be less than good? In my opinion, this happens because even good people with good intentions have egos, and the ego's aim is always some form of personal enhancement. The self-proclaimed "seekers of truth" often have personal superiority as their unconscious agenda. Invariably, they end up convincing themselves that they have attained it. Those who think of themselves as normal and equal, and who are quite aware of their many limitations, simply are not tempted to believe that they personally can discover a spiritual truth that other people are unaware of. Yet, by definition, that is what a "seeker of truth" believes.

Although most individuals start a spiritual path out of their yearning to be good, often they gradually begin to move in the opposite direction. The more time they put into talking, studying, and arguing about their path, the more self-absorbed they become. They often end up less flexible and less forgiving than they were when they first started!

Rather than oneness, what they actually learn is how to mask their unhealed mind, act spiritual, and make their thoughts less conscious. In addition, they accumulate hundreds of new spiritual concepts, which, unfortunately, are the primary standards by which the devout are judged (as well as TV pundits, columnists, politicians, nonfiction authors, talking-head experts, and the like.). All the while, they seem unaware that these changes are occurring.

In lieu of *true* enlightenment, many spiritually correct people make an unconscious determination that they have arrived. Or, they decide that they have come close enough to the end of the journey that the remaining distance is of no consequence and requires very little of their attention. Only if they are lucky, or if they face some rude awakening, do they come to terms with the fact that their worst impulses have been growing in power and influence over them.

Having seen this dynamic operate in ourselves and others countless times, Gayle and I now put far greater emphasis on exposing the ways the ego takes over spiritual efforts. The fact is, the day you started your spiritual path, your ego started it also, and for every spiritual motive you have, there is an ego motive as well. This is not reason to be afraid, but it is reason to be acutely aware.

Those individuals we know intimately and whom we believe are close to being awake seem to have no interest in contrasting themselves with other people. Generally speaking, they live simple, ordinary lives. They are comfortable to be around. Their time is usually devoted to unimportant things and their hearts to "unimportant" people. They have no inflexible concepts or rigid habits, and there is nothing particularly unusual about the subjects they choose to talk about or anything outstanding about their personal mannerisms. They are easily pleased, and usually they are happy for no apparent reason. Because their own egos are no longer destructive, they find other people's egos amusing and endearing. Above all, they are equal and familiar. They would not be good subjects for a magazine profile. Yet, into the mundane, everyday circumstances of their lives, they quietly pour their comfort and their peace.

How could one person's way possibly be superior to another person's way if God is leading us all?

Letting Go of "Spiritual" Laws of Success

As a people, until the 1960s we didn't believe in metaphysical laws or "universal principles" so much as we believed in the one great Game Plan: If you did "what was right." If you didn't question "authority," your place in society, or the status quo. If you didn't lie, swear, cheat, or "drink to excess." If you worked long hours and saved your money so that some day you could pass it on to your children. If you were loyal to your country, the company you worked for, the political party of your family, and your alma mater. If you performed your duties as a housewife or a "provider." If you attended your house of worship and tithed regularly. Then "everything would work out" and at some point you would walk into the sunset.

This unquestioned approach to life extended even to one's personal choice in car companies, the dress styles of the day, and one's taste in music and movie stars. The key was sticking to "the plan," which everyone more or less understood and agreed on. As a culture, we were surprisingly consistent in our adherence to this approach. We told each other stories of the rewards of people who "worked hard and lived by the rules." We cherished examples of what happened to those who didn't.

No one felt a need to uncover the laws of love or success because our society thought it already knew "how to conduct yourself" in ways that allowed one's life to work out. That it was possible for life to work out and that "everything adds up" was never questioned.

Then along came the Vietnam War and doubt began pouring into our cultural psyche. Within a remarkably few years, we no longer believed in a single game plan, and at the start of the twenty-first century we have come close to assuming that acting counter to "the way things are done" gives you a better chance at happiness than walking "the path most traveled." Now devotion can turn you into a "caregiver"; your family can "enable" you to fail; your children can impede "your dreams"; your company, your religion, and the political leaders you last voted for can fail to "meet your needs." You should feel free to experiment with different "lifestyles" and "exotic" forms of entertainment. You should be as open to switching friends and family members as you are to changing your job, location, or hairstyle.

Although it was inevitable that we would begin to challenge the cherished "strengths" of our society, we have paid a heavy price for going beyond merely questioning our values to obsessively undermining them. We have focused so strongly on doubting our former approach to life that doubt has become an end in itself. Most of us find that we can no longer look at anything without anxiety, uncertainty, and cynicism. The average person can't even sit down and eat a simple meal without conflict.

Understandably, we now long to know what *can* be counted on, what the basic forces and facts *are*. If the old way doesn't get us the life we want, what will? We hunger to know the rules and we want them spelled out and numbered.

Fortunately, this will never happen. If it could, we would be locked forever in an unfair and loveless reality.

> The key to release and freedom is the recognition that the world doesn't work, not the continued search for a magic formula.

After thousands of years of looking for them, it should be obvious there are no hidden laws. The world simply is not governed by a philosophy, doctrine, or set of rules. No one's life is predictable, solvable, or even reasonable. Once we acknowledge this, a great and totally unnecessary burden is lifted from our shoulders.

Unquestionably, many writers and teachers claim to have discovered the laws of happiness and success. But no one agrees on precisely what these are. It's also curious that in our culture, it is close to being a tradition that our religious and spiritual leaders seldom practice what they preach, which raises the following question: Do they *really* believe they have discovered the laws of happiness and success?

Why would we even want such laws? Isn't it because we think the key to happiness is to change the people and circumstances around us? We insanely believe that the key to peace is war. Yet as soon as we try to control anything, we split our mind and lose our sense of inner comfort. We can change what we *bring* to the people and circumstances surrounding us, but we can't dominate them.

Perhaps the only approach that comes remotely close to a rule of life is that when you are relaxed and flexible, you are happy; when you are rigid and controlling, you are unhappy. Therefore, the key is actually to *let go* of our urge to get people to behave and events to go our way.

No matter how experienced the psychologist, how learned the theologian, how wise the philosopher, or how holy the saint, none of them can control a two-year-old. Who among us can even predict the weather? As someone said to me recently, "The next time you think there is some situation you can control, try doing it when you have diarrhea."

The simple fact is that you and I don't control the tiniest events of our lives. Despite repeated New Year's resolutions, most members of the human species can't even turn down a donut. Thus the idea of controlling our partner, teenager, in-laws, or supervisor is ludicrous.

It's interesting that the great spiritual teachers of the past did not control outcomes. Jesus couldn't even get his disciples to stay awake for an hour—although he tried twice! What made these teachers great was that they devoted themselves to the people before them wholly and constantly—even though the results were disappointing. In contrast, you and I have limited patience and "can only do so much." If the picture doesn't change, we bail out.

> Notice that the moment you become unhappy is usually the moment you attempt to control another person.

Most people think they know the pieces that make up the puzzle of their life. They believe that they already have a few of them resting quietly in place, and all they have to do is get the rest of them to fit. However, even the ones that momentarily fit are changing shape and soon will not fit, and to those that float just out of reach, new ones are forever being added. No one's life, including the lives of saints and ascended masters, finally gets ironed out and runs smoothly.

Jesus, the Buddha, Gandhi, Martin Luther King, Jr., and Mother Teresa's *approach* to life is thought by many to have come close to perfection. If theirs was not a flawless approach, certainly it was about as good as it gets. Yet even their lives often did not go well. If that is true of individuals who by the end of their lives lived impeccably, then nothing you or I do with our minds or bodily habits can force our lives to run well.

Would we want such an outcome even if we could have it? For example, do you *want* more money than other people? Whom would you choose to have less? Do you *want* to be a person who never dies? Whom would you choose to be the ones who do? Do you truly *want* your teenager under your control? If so, which moments will she live the role that you assign to her and which moments will she choose for herself?

We can't all have financial superiority, super health, a great romance, unbelievable sex, and so forth, because those states exist in comparison. One of numerous reasons we never reach the place where everything is the way we want it is that all attainments fluctuate in contrast to other attainments. Every level of achievement fades before the unremitting parade of new comparisons. You save your money and get a better car, but for how long is it a "better" car? You trade in your old spouse for a better one, but for how long is he or she "better"? You work hard at the spa and get in better shape, but you don't remain in "better" shape in either your mind or anyone else's.

Letting Go of Our Personal Struggle

Unless our mind is flexible, we are restricted to old fears and yearnings and experience only reactions we had before. If we have already decided what we will like and dislike, or who is worthy of love and who is not, we have blocked the experience of an all-encompassing peace. The mind is the door to the heart. It can make entering the Place of Beauty complicated or simple, depending on how we use it.

We never need fear our thoughts, because we are the ones who think them. We are free to change our line of thought—our mental orientation, our reality preference—anytime we choose. It's as simple as gripping the wheel tightly and looking down at the road, or gripping it easily and looking out at the road. The road remains the same, but we can drive it hard or light.

Thoughts that pick over and critique each superficial characteristic of our own and other people's personalities are sticky and move haltingly and uncomfortably. Thoughts that take in each person as a whole and are quick to understand move easily and lightly. An open mind does not have lists of censored subjects. Its texture is peace, and its aim is to think about whatever subject is before it with ease.

It is true that we have choices about what we say and do. It is also true that when our level of learning changes, this growth is reflected in the decisions we make. Given our level of learning at the time we made almost any choice, if we could somehow return to the point of decision, we would probably choose the same.

You may have reached the time in your life when you can watch with some degree of amusement these points of decision come and go—whether to get up now or press the snooze button, what to put on, what to eat for breakfast, how to react to the driver who hasn't seen the light change. You watch yourself choose and you know that you could choose differently, but by now you are sufficiently familiar with the chaos of the world that you wait in peace and watch with interest to see what comes next.

Furthermore, you see that this level of decision making isn't very meaningful. Meaning lies in your heart's intent. Choices flow more from the deeper desires than from a conscious decision-making process. If your heart's intent is oneness and joining, your choices become more effortless and automatic.

This is especially apparent as we begin experiencing a deeper degree of spiritual oneness with the people around us, and especially in our primary relationships. Feeling another's pain or peace as if it were our own, we now have no choice but to respond from love. Parents who feel at one with their children, for example, may wonder why they continue making endless sacrifices for them. They may even chide themselves for being such pushovers, yet they keep on sacrificing. Failing to make even the smallest of these sacrifices eventually becomes spiritually impossible. Their mere hesitancy to do so throws them into immediate conflict and emotional pain.

Naturally, the separation psychology of our day looks down on this. In fact, it is classified as a sickness. Nevertheless, when you see yourself in another, you will act in the best interests of that person, and very often those who observe you do this will not understand.

As we continue our spiritual journey, it becomes clear why Jesus, Gandhi, Martin Luther King, Jr., and others— knowing in advance that to keep doing what they were doing would mean their deaths—proceeded anyway. Today, many authorities would think of this as not just sick but psychotic. Yet these men were not naive or unaware, and they certainly were not insane. They were walking a spiritual path rather than a worldly one, and the twists and turns of the worldly path had become relatively unimportant to them.

> *Our spiritual progress is often indicated by our willingness to stop fiddling with our personal lives. This allows us to see relationship. Relationship, it turns out, was always there. We just didn't notice.*

Notwithstanding the legends of the great martyrs, letting go of our lives puts us in less danger, rather than more. We merely lose interest in micro-management, but the decisions we make about our health, safety, and finances are more peaceful and more loving of ourselves. We accept our spouses, children, friends, pets, and our bodies as they are and commit deeply to them. We don't need a new spouse or new friends in order to commit, because now we know that commitment itself trans-forms us. And yet, commitment often will not change other egos and iron out difficulties.

Obviously, this doesn't mean that we adopt the rule of never changing anything. *Change is not somehow less spiritual than no change*. But our urge to tinker with circumstance lessens as our focus on the eternal sharpens. When we make a change, now we do so because we see a simpler way of maintaining our focus. Questions such as the following can help make each decision an aid to our concentration:

"What will complicate my life the least?"

"What is my peaceful preference?"

"Will this help me enjoy my loved ones more?"

"Am I conflicted about what to do?—Then I will wait."

"What decision will I later chew on the least?"

If our weight is distracting us, we lose some weight. If it isn't, we don't. If another job would be less distracting, we change jobs, perhaps even if it means a pay cut. If getting a higher paying job would simplify our life and is an option open to us, we may make this change.

Half of Gayle's and my income used to come from the workshops and talks we gave around the country, but when it became clear that traveling as much as we did was not good for our children, we stopped. When one of their girls was getting caught up in a highly destructive relationship with a neighborhood girl, a family we know sold their dream home and moved into a less desirable house in a less desirable part of town.

Remarkably little of this kind of adjustment has to be made by anyone. With most people, no dramatic life change is called for, and if they are well along on their journey, they no longer make changes just to be making them.

We must let our day, our week, our life come to us, rather than ceaselessly clawing to get the life we want. Instead of focusing on what hasn't been done for us, we must look more gently on the particular circumstances we find ourselves in at the moment and concentrate on experiencing stillness and peace where we are.

Poppie

When I met him, Poppie was four and still couldn't talk. A year before, an operation had released his tongue from the base of his mouth, and although his eyes were bright with intelligence, he was still in the preverbal stage of a one-year-old. He chattered almost musically, but in nonsensical sounds.

His parents, both preoccupied with their careers, kept him upstairs in rooms filled with toys but devoid of other humans. However, now that he was approaching school age, they were suddenly concerned that their child wasn't normal.

The father was a "wildcatter," which meant he drilled oil wells in unproven locations, often requiring him to get little or no sleep for days at a time. After returning home he would often sleep two or three days in a row. When he woke, he would verbally abuse his wife, then go back to the oilfields.

My answer to their question of whether Poppie was normal was from a spiritual standpoint. I pointed out that he played normally and laughed often. I especially singled out his deep bond with his dog. The mother and father had gotten him a German Shepherd puppy, and they soon discovered that Poppie was a lot less trouble if they left the dog with him upstairs and simply had the housekeeper clean up the dog's messes.

Although Poppie lived upstairs with his dog, he could hear when his mother was being yelled at, and later, when he could talk, he told me that he had long been in the habit of coming quietly down the stairs to "watch the fights." "She probably deserves it," he told me. Knowing that about the only times she spoke to Poppie were to yell at him, I could understand his childlike sense of justice.

Poppie had come into the family in a most unusual way. One day the father had walked over to a shack that he had noticed some distance from one of his wells. He opened the door, and there on a plank floor was a ten-month-old baby playing in his own excrement behind a crude fence. He called the authorities and was later told that the child belonged to a prostitute who had kept him hidden since birth. Every day she would bring him food and water, then leave.

A lawyer was hired; the mother was paid off; and eventually Poppie was legally adopted. But from Poppie's standpoint, he merely went from one form of isolation to another. Of course, he didn't know he was isolated—it was the only life he had ever had.

One day I decided to take Poppie out for a day of fun. By then he was five and a half and was talking just fine. We first went to a city park with slides, swing sets, and the like. Poppie noticed a gigantic sandbox and ran toward it. As I got closer, I saw that what I thought from a distance were kids playing, was really a group of young adults with Down syndrome who obviously were there from some group home for an outing.

The symptoms they exhibited were fairly severe. These included the usual facial characteristics and slurred speech, but some of them also drooled or had runny noses that they didn't wipe. The park was in one of the wealthier neighborhoods of the city and I noticed that no other parent or babysitter was allowing their child to get near the sandbox.

As almost everyone knows, individuals with Down syndrome pose no danger to other people. Their congenital condition is not contagious, nor are they prone to violence. As a group they actually tend to be less violent and noticeably happier. Yet the other adults there that day not only weren't letting their children play with the Down adults—even though a couple of the smaller kids clearly wanted to—they seemed to be averting their eyes.

Poppie played with this loud and exuberant group until they had to leave, and although we went to several other places that are thought to be more impressive than a city park—a marine park and the beach—at the end of the day, Poppie asked me when we could go back and "play with those funny guys."

Letting Go of Perfection

Going through a single day is like being in a spaceship passing among heavenly bodies. Each mass, small and large, has its gravitational pull and most travelers shift directions continuously. Notice how little it takes for us to get off course. There is a great difference, though, between straying occasionally from the inner course we have set for ourselves and having no course other than the values hawked by the voices from the surrounding asylum.

If they saw it happen, everything we do today would be called a mistake by at least one columnist, two relatives, three former schoolteachers, four authorities on TV, five religious leaders, and every talk show audience that ever listened to radio or TV. Yet if we did it all differently, about the same numbers would agree we were still mistaken. So what should we do? Nothing? No, that too would be a mistake—because it would be a reaction, not a purpose. We would still be a victim of all the dissonant voices that call out to us. If we act with no sense of heart or inner direction, the outcome can hold nothing of lasting value, nothing that can lift up a loved one or nourish our soul.

It's never possible to "get it right" or "make it happen," and when that is our focus, we are valuing the wrong outcome. Perfection isn't found in "the way things go." Yet it's always possible to act from peace by making peace our aim.

What if we were to withhold finality and instead looked on all things with open-ended interest? What if we were consistent about what we are but tentative about what we saw? If we could say to ourselves, "Today, I will have flexible eyes. I will plant myself strongly within the decision to look softly. I will move through the day as if it had never occurred before. I will set no judgment in place ahead of time. Over and over, I will return to the fact that I have not had *this* particular day before. I have never had *this* phone conversation, been in *this* crowd, looked at *this* sky, had *this* sensation. I will observe how everyone and every circumstance is a little different now than they have ever been. Each difference I see today will be a prize I collect—and by the end of the day, I will be wealthy in newness."

 release 23

Suggested time: 1 or more days

You need keep only one thought before your mind. As you go through the day, say to yourself,

"Below my usual reactions, is the quietness of my heart.

Below the chaos of the world, is the wholeness of God's peace."

Letting Go

For most of us, the word *oneness* is gibberish. Perhaps it's a concept with a nice ring, but it refers to nothing real in our experience. When we hear ideas such as, "We will all awaken to our oneness in God," many of us think of spiritual reality as a huge blended drink in which all our distinctions are whipped into sameness and we as individuals cease to exist.

The affection we have for each other unquestionably heads toward oneness or unity, but whom do you know who has arrived? Quite naturally, in a world where all things are known by their differences, we believe that finding those people who are *less* different (more like us) is the key to strong friendship and loving partnership. People sometimes say of a rocky association, "We have our differences." The rationale that "we discovered we had little in common" is considered sufficient grounds for ending a marriage or breaking up a friendship. For some guardians or parents, "not fitting in" is grounds for turning against one of their biological children, "disrupting" an adoption, or giving back a foster child.

Because there is no eternal oneness in the world, we strive for an impression, an intimation of oneness. In the classified "personals" and in our encounters with strangers, we seek the common ground. In the little conversations we have with a clerk, a waiter, or a stranger standing in line, we often try to say something "agreeable." Weather, for example, is considered a "safe subject"—meaning we are less likely to seem too different if we stick to temperature and rain. That is, provided we don't go deeply into our *personal* feelings about weather. If we start recounting a childhood rain trauma to a toll-both operator, it's a safe bet we won't achieve a sense of bonding.

If we wish to *maintain* a relationship with a relative or friend, we usually stick to "areas of agreement." Perhaps an adult daughter finds that she gets along with her mother best when they are in the kitchen. An adult son notices that things go more smoothly with his father when they watch "the game" together. Most people know which friendships can be hurt by a political or religious discussion and avoid those topics.

Naturally, we believe this is the reality we must settle for. If we are to have a small measure of love and belonging, of being welcomed and accepted, we must carefully balance each relationship on the little edge of common ground we have with those individuals. Yet the more experiences we have, the more precarious we realize this balance is. If we look closely—and certainly the present ideal is to scrutinize all relationships—we see that we are different from every person we know in all respects. We try to put a good face on this by saying that variety is the spice of life. Yet regardless of how we rationalize it, loneliness remains the world's dominant emotion. We came into the world alone. We will leave it alone. And while we are here, we are *wholly* united with no living thing, not even ourselves.

In the last few decades of the twentieth century, through television and other forms of mass communication, we became dramatically more aware of people's circumstances throughout the world. Many of us began to feel overwhelmed and suffocated by the enormity of humanity's misery. Shangri-la and the magical land of the Hobbits obviously wasn't out there. We now knew all too well what was out there.

At the time this was happening on a worldwide scale, it also was occurring within the intimate details of our lives. Distance, time, and routine once provided barriers and breathing space, but now the little difficulties and problems of our friends and coworkers began to crowd into our evenings, weekends, and vacations with the advent of cell phones, pagers, e-mail, voice messaging, and the "Evernet."

Thus we began to emphasize, even to cherish, our differences as a means of escaping each other. We broke our intact families into single-parent families, our large nations into smaller ones, our religions into sects, our political parties into "wings," our news commentaries into "opposing" commentaries, and our talk shows into opinion shows.

Whether we are seeking closer relationships or trying to buffer ourselves from human misery, only two options seem to be available: We can choose more difference or less difference. What we can't choose is love. We can't choose it because we doubt it. We don't trust it because nothing in our experience consistently reflects it. Yet even as our disbelief in love hardens, our longing for it grows.

It's interesting that during this period when we find it so difficult to offer welcome and a sense of home to other members of our human family—even to our own mates and children—there is also a growing homesickness within the hearts of so many. This Welcome, this Embrace that we long for, I call

God. I have no better reason for using that word than my own familiarity with it and the comfort I feel when I silently say it. Yet I think of it as a mere indicator of a vast Splendor that is nearer to us than our breath and so utterly harmless that it could be feared by no living thing. It is Love, the great Joy and indescribable Wholeness that enfolds us all, and it can be experienced merely by letting go of everything that is not Love.

I therefore invite you to let go of your doubts and misgivings and take a leap of faith. Release your fears, your hopes, and your life into the hands of the One who is with you now, who has never left you and never will leave you, who wants only your happiness and peace. If you were thrown beyond time and space, this Friend would already be there to welcome and comfort you. For this is the Friend you have known ever since you were a little child.

In each of the encounters we have throughout the day, we leave something behind. In our wake people feel either more relaxed or more separate, more seen or more ignored, more peaceful or more conflicted. And every time someone comes to mind, either we send forth our comfort or our doubt, our blessing or our judgment. If we wish to know the One who is Love, we must extend love past the boundaries of our ego. But how is this done if not moment by moment, gesture by gesture? Only by giving the tiny miracles of understanding, support, forbearance, and happiness can we know Love.

Neither words nor silence have much to do with these miracles. The sincerity of our heart is the power behind them. For where is Family and Home if not within the ocean of our relationships? Where else can the presence of God first be felt? In the words of the old Shaker hymn, "If you love not one another in daily communion, how can you love God whom you have never seen? If you love one another, then God is within you, and you are made pure to live in the light."

Love is not joining with some shining concept in the sky.

It is joining with each other. It is lived and expressed in the errands, tasks, and chance meetings that fill each day. Instant by instant we choose to see our sameness and equality with others. We choose to recognize the familiar in each heart. By loving, we wake to Love. By extending peace, we wake to Peace.

In your journey, you have valued many things, but now your heart and your treasure are becoming one. Do not doubt that the One who is with you will give you Everything, if you will merely let go of everything else.

Releases

Thirty Days of Letting-Go Practices

The most productive approach is to take each Release in order and do it for the suggested number of days before going to the next one. Naturally, the discussion of ideas leading up to and following each Release can be read and reread at any pace that is comfortable.

release 1	1 day	20
release 2	1 day	28
release 3	1 day	37
release 4	1 day	52
release 5	2 days	63
release 6	1 day	68
release 7	2 days	78
release 8	2 days	79
release 9	Extra Credit, Extra Release	92
release 10	A Key Release 4 days	97
release 11	2 days	110
release 12	2 days	111
release 13	1 day	111
release 14	1 day	124
release 15	1 day	126
release 16	A Special Needs Release	130
release 17	1 day	137
release 18	2 days	146
release 19	1 day	159
release 20	1 day	183
release 21	1 day	190
release 22	1 day	192
release 23	1 day	213

About the Author

Hugh Prather is the author of more than fourteen books, including the bestselling *Notes to Myself, Spiritual Notes to Myself, Notes on How to Live in the World...And Still Be Happy, Spiritual Parenting,* and *I Will Never Leave You.* He lives with Gayle, his wife of thirty-three years, in Tucson, Arizona, where he is the resident minister at St. Francis in the Foothills United Methodist Church. Prather is also the host of "Living in the Light" on the Wisdom Radio Network and Webcast. He and Gayle also write monthly columns for Beliefnet and for The Connection magazine.

To Our Readers

CONARI PRESS publishes books on topics ranging from spirituality, personal growth, and relationships to women's issues, parenting, and social issues. Our mission is to publish quality books that will make a difference in people's lives—how we feel about ourselves and how we relate to one another. We value integrity, compassion, and receptivity, both in the books we publish and in the way we do business.

As a member of the community, we sponsor the Random Acts of Kindness™ Foundation, the guiding force behind Random Acts of Kindness™ Week. We donate our damaged books to nonprofit organizations, dedicate a portion of our proceeds from certain books to charitable causes, and continually look for new ways to use natural resources as wisely as possible.

Our readers are our most important resource, and we value your input, suggestions, and ideas about what you would like to see published. Please feel free to contact us, to request our latest book catalog, or to be added to our mailing list.

Conari Press

An imprint of Red Wheel/Weiser, llc

P.O. Box 612

Yoek Beach, ME 03910-0612

800-423-7087

www.conari.com